RICHARD DYER, CHRISTINE GERAGHTY, MARION JORDAN,
TERRY LOVELL, RICHARD PATERSON, JOHN STEWART

CORONATION STREET

of Further and Higher Education
GUILDFORD COLLEGE

1981
BFI Publishing

791.456 DYE

88814

THE AUTHORS

Richard Dyer is a Lecturer in Film Studies at the University of Warwick. His publications include *Stars* (BFI) and *Heavenly Bodies* (Macmillan) and BFI Education Department Study Guides on *Stars* and *Marilyn Monroe*. He edited *Gays and Film*, and has contributed to *Gay Left* and *Movie*. He is involved in various aspects of the gay movement. *Christine Geraghty* is a NALGO branch administrator and lectures on the University of London Film Studies Diploma course. She was a long-standing member of the SEFT Executive and a founder member of the Women and Film Study Group. She has written for *Movie*. *Marion Jordan* has taught Russian and English and was a founder member of the Keele SEFT Group. *Terry Lovell* is a Lecturer in Sociology at the University of Warwick. She is the author of *Pictures of Reality: Aesthetics, Politics and Pleasure*, has contributed to *Sociology of Literature* and *Sociology of Mass Communications*, and written for *Screen*. She was also a founder member of the Women and Film Study Group. *Richard Paterson* is Television Projects Officer at the BFI and is co-editor (with Phillip Drummond) of *Television in Transition*. *John Stewart* is the BFI Television Access Officer and has contributed to *Screen Education*.

Published by the British Film Institute
127 Charing Cross Road
London WC2H OEA
Copyright © British Film Institute 1981
Individual contributions Copyright © the authors

British Library Cataloguing in Publication Data
Coronation Street. – (BFI TV Monograph; no. 13)
1. Television plays
I. Dyer, Richard
791.45'72 PN 1992.77.C/

ISBN 0 85170 110 8

Reprinted 1987

Printed in Great Britain by Jason Press Ltd, Hertford

Contents

Acknowledgments

The authors would like to thank the following people for their co-operation in this project: Gordon McKellar, Bill Podmore, Eric Rosser and Jane Lawrence of Granada Television; Jimmy Royle of Independent Television Publications; Jackie Winterbottom and Margaret Hennessey, and Erich Sargeant for the still photography, of the BFI.

Thanks are also due to the other members of both the Women and Film Study Group and the Keele SEFT Group for their invaluable contributions through discussion and comment, and particularly to Stephanie McKnight of the former, who was largely responsible, with Christine Geraghty, for the initiation of the publication.

RICHARD DYER

Introduction

This set of essays on *Coronation Street* is primarily concerned with wider
issues in understanding television than its title might suggest. *Coronation
Street* is an example, a point of departure and of reference. It represents one
of broadcasting's most typical forms, the continuous serial. Although potentially available as a vehicle for any kind of fictional world, in practice the
continuous serial, a form only known on radio and television, has restricted
itself to one such world, that usually designated 'everyday life' or 'family
drama' and labelled as the province of 'soap-opera'. *Coronation Street* has
been one of the two most successful soap operas on British television, the
other being *Crossroads*. It is thus both typical of soap opera and a supreme
realisation of its popular and/or commercial potential.

However, these essays are not solely concerned with *Coronation Street* as
continuous soap opera at the narrow level of broadcasting specificity. They
also address issues concerning the nature of popular/mass culture. They
examine both what kinds of things *Coronation Street* says and can say – the
representational discourse of *Coronation Street*, of soap opera, if you will; and
also the kinds of pleasurable experience *Coronation Street* offers its viewers.
Before further considering these two themes, at once in opposition and
complementary to each other, I should like first to discuss what is perhaps
an absence in these writings, namely, the choice of *Coronation Street* as object.

The purposes behind these essays are the wider ones outlined above. But
why *Coronation Street*? Why not *Crossroads*, more successful and more
continuous? All the essays certainly see *Crossroads*, *The Archers* and other
soap operas and series as important points of reference, yet *Coronation Street*
remains the focus. To take one series as a focus is a proper intellectual
limitation, yet the choice of *Coronation Street* is not 'innocent'. There is quite a
lot at stake in its choice.

It would be wrong to ignore altogether what is assuredly a factor in the
choice, namely, the widespread feeling among those who write on the media
that *Coronation Street* is somehow 'better' than its soap opera peers. This
admiration for the series is most clearly conveyed in Marion Jordan's essay,
but it certainly informs the other essays as well as the very choice of *Coronation Street* in the first place. Yet the writers refrain from affirming what is in
practice very widely maintained, that *Coronation Street* is better written,
better acted, better staged and better constructed (as narrative) than, particularly, *Crossroads*. Many of the effects of representation and of pleasure in
the series are sustained and even constituted by these factors. I do not raise
this here in order to sneak in through the back door easy, unproblematised

1

notions as to what constitutes 'good' television, a 'good' performance, a 'good' script. We should rather be asking what is meant by the label 'good' in these contexts. What qualities are so designated, and what social, moral and aesthetic values are inscribed in them? Does the fact that *Coronation Street* has a particular critical following – though the exact nature and extent of this can only be guessed at – merely derive from the particular class and gender positions occupied by the critics, or do we need to get up the nerve to suggest that evaluative work could have some intellectual legitimacy if rigorously pursued? As it is, evaluation is constantly ushered in unrigorously, whether it be in the inexorable pull of classic Hollywood for the many varieties of structuralist analysis or the endless attempt to pin down progressive texts in the case of more political writers.

But let us leave this embarrassing terrain and focus on a more narrow aspect of the choice of *Coronation Street*. The series lays claim to being 'about' working-class culture and is also marked by the presence of strong and positive female characters. It thus supplies social images that are conspicuous for their rarity on British television, and that are necessarily of particular interest to anyone working within broadly Marxist and/or feminist perspectives, as is the case in this book.

It is important to remind ourselves that *Coronation Street* came out of a particular moment in British cultural history, a moment most strikingly and decisively marked by Richard Hoggart's book, *The Uses of Literacy* (1957). This book, together with other sociological works and novels, as well as films and theatre, was concerned to 'discover' and legitimate a tradition of culture that could authentically be termed 'working-class'. *The Uses of Literacy* was a best seller, not comparable to a Harold Robbins or an Agatha Christie, but certainly by academic standards. Its influence at all levels of institutionalised cultural practice was enormous, and its influence on education, especially the teaching of English, has led to generations of people brought up with some version of its reigning notions. Four things are of particular importance in the inflection Hoggart gave to the definition of working-class culture, and we can trace the relation of each to the wider media appropriation of the book, as well as to *Coronation Street* in particular.

First, Hoggart understood culture in an essentially anthropological sense, not as the artistic product of a given group of people but as patterns of interaction, sets of assumptions, ways of getting along together. What he set out to describe was the 'common sense' of 'everyday life' for the working class, in a way that both caught the apparent naturalness, down-to-earth, air-that-you-breathe feeling of such notions and yet acknowledged the specificity of the actual content of common sense. There is enormous difficulty here, since common sense is both 'wise' in its negotiation of the immediate business of living yet 'blinkered' in its inability to see beyond or above the immediate. There has been a renewed interest in this way of understanding common sense in recent years due to the revival of interest in the ideas of Antonio Gramsci. Hoggart's approach is less political, less

Marxist, than Gramsci's but his treatment of common sense is none the less extremely nuanced. Yet, like so many aspects of the book, only one side of the coin was taken. The recognition of the strengths and weaknesses of common sense was read as an unqualified celebration of it. Hoggart's listings of salty aphorisms, his references to the 'full, rich life' of charabanc outings, aspidistras and pub singsongs were appropriated as a reconfirmation of a long-standing belief in the ebullient cornucopia of low-life existence. What now looked exaggerated in Dickens and formalised in music-hall was re-read as authentic through Hoggart's beautifully written personal account of working-class life.

It has often been pointed out that the supreme weakness of Hoggart's book, its glaring absence, is the virtual exclusion of all reference to the political and work institutions of the working class (for example, Critcher, 1979). Labour activists of all kinds are marginalised into one paragraph referring to their untypicality and there is no account of any kind of paid working life. Thus although Hoggart focuses on the working class, the very thing that defines that class as a class – their work (in its relation to the means of production of life in capitalist society) – is missing. Class becomes *only* a matter of life-style, value-systems.

It is interesting to remember that Hoggart's book appeared alongside the 'embourgeoisement thesis', which argued that the specific character of the working class, especially in a period of improved wages, strong unions and the widespread availability of consumer durables, was gradually being eroded so that we were all becoming middle class in our attitudes, values and way of life. One riposte to this thesis, with impressive sociological evidence to back it up (Goldthorpe, 1968-9), was that wages, unions and consumerism did not alter the fundamental relation of the working class to capital and the core of values founded upon that relation. Hoggart's book took a different tack. Working-class values stemmed from the particular historical formation of the home and community life of the working class. These were under threat, especially from the mass media and *a fortiori* television, but if there was resistance to embourgeoisement it was not because of the working class' relation to capital but because of its essential character. Hoggart thus upheld the notion of class and the specificity of working-class culture while at the same time depoliticising them.

Thirdly, Hoggart's stress on home and community meant a stress on women. Once again, his account is nuanced. He recognises how very hard the brunt of domestic labour falls on women and their strength and endurance in the face of it; yet he also draws the most glowing portrait of the warmth of the working-class mother, while offering any number of strikingly sentimental moral asides upon the mores of young working-class women. And, once again, the appropriation of the book takes out the nuances, plays down the hardship and the moralism, plays up the strength and warmth. There is in *The Uses of Literacy* no awareness of the economic role of domestic labour, of the effect of patriarchal traditions in the organisation of domesticity and sexuality, themes that have had a much greater centrality in political and intellectual life in the last decade. Given the book's date, their absence is less striking than the absence of labour politics, though one should note that in a comparable, though less successful, book of the period, *Coal is Our Life* (Dennis, 1969), there is a surprisingly acute sense of the operations of gender within and across working-class culture.

Finally, Hoggart's description of working-class culture focuses on his own upbringing in the 1930s and, as has already been mentioned, is partly concerned with conducting a polemic against the erosion of this culture by the mass media. This backwards look, together with finding the past prefer-able to the present, inevitably makes it hard not to read the book as nostalgic. I say 'hard not to' because in fact Hoggart is careful to say on many occasions that he is not concerned to upgrade the past, that he does recognise the appalling suffering of the working class in the 30s and before. Yet the dominant reading of the book, and the accusation most often levelled against it, is that it is nostalgic.

It is easy to see how these four aspects of *The Uses of Literacy* – the emphasis on common sense, the absence of work and politics, the stress on women and the strength of women, and the perspective of nostalgia – inform *Coronation Street* and indeed come close to defining its fictional world. (There are even more precise connections, with figures and images from *The Uses of Literacy* appearing in early episodes of *Coronation Street* – the scholarship boy [Ken Barlow];* watching television and reading particular newspapers as indi-cators of fecklessness [the Tanners, now the Ogdens]; the ambivalent class position of publicans; the plethora of splendid mums.)

Coronation Street takes as its mode the interactions of everyday life as realised in common-sense speech and philosophy. The narrative may take more un-everyday events as its focus, the multiplicity of marriages, deaths, disappearances and so on for which soap opera is so often derided. Yet in *Coronation Street* at least these are always enacted within the mode of com-mon sense, which is to say that they are also understood and contained by common sense. However, the common sense of *Coronation Street* is that of a particular description in a particular moment (*The Uses of Literacy*), whose truth is guaranteed by being based on personal testimony. In this way the peculiarity of the common sense has been naturalised, which gives it a special authority as a solvent of troublesome issues or perspectives.

The other links between *Coronation Street* and *The Uses of Literacy* may be quickly outlined. 'Life' in *Coronation Street* – though here it is important to bear in mind Christine Geraghty's analysis of soap opera conventions at least as much as the *Coronation Street/Uses of Literacy* nexus – is defined as community, interpersonal activity on a day-to-day basis. Work is seldom shown and, when it is, is treated in terms of styles of personal interaction

---

* This is also a constant of a certain strain of working-class fiction, e.g. *How Green Is My Valley, The Stars Look Down*, etc.

4

(e.g. the gossip of the women at Mike Baldwin's factory, the joking relation-ship between staff and customers in the Rovers Return). Women characters have always been consistently emphasised, a point Marion Jordan substanti-ates in her essay; and the nostalgic cast of the serial is unmistakable. This was most explicit in the period when the credit sequence was based on a camera zoom from a long shot of a high-rise block of flats to a close-up of a back-to-back street, from the impersonality of modern planned architec-ture to the human scale of the old working-class street.

Coronation Street came out of the moment of *The Uses of Literacy* and is arguably still caught up in it. Thus what is important about it – its central focus on working-class life and on strong female characters – is still held in the particular way of setting up ideas and images of the working class' and women that are crystallised and given a new lease of life in *The Uses of Literacy*. The serial has evolved, but – and here we need more sustained analysis to support or disprove what I'm going to say – its way of realising class and gender remains unchanged. Thus even though it does sometimes show paid work, does acknowledge the role of domestic labour and ine-qualities between the sexes, can be explicit about wider issues, nevertheless these extensions of subject matter have not really altered the content of the series. Common sense, constructed as a sensible and obvious refusal of wider perspectives, is always at hand to be the vehicle for the resolution of problems, however considerable their implications. Class as materially determined in relation to the means of production, and much less as self-realised in political and social action, is still either absent or (often comically) marginalised. Women's strength and endurance is celebrated, but as the inevitable and given lot of women rather than as socially deter-minant. The nostalgic tone of the serial consigns any lingering effective class consciousness to something that, to all intents and purposes, is in the past.

This is not to deny the very real strengths of the serial, rather it is to characterise its particular mode and to offer some very sketchy account of its historicity. It may be that what is particular to *Coronation Street* is *also* what is valuable about it. The affirmation of common sense must always put a brake on any theory or politics that does not connect at all with the lived texture of everyday life. The concentration on community and interpersonal interac-tion certainly counters the reduction of class to paid positions in the economic base, and the acknowledgment of female strength and endurance must be welcome in the context of the nincompoops that pass for the representation of women in most television. Even the nostalgia allows for a certain utopianism, which is to say the assertion of a vivid image of how life should be. I do not propose to argue at length here the legitimacy of utopian imagery in art,* and certainly the nostalgic cast of *Coronation Street* may undermine its utopian impulse by discounting it as a thing past. None the

* For discussion of the place of utopianism in Marxist theory of art, see Maynard Solomon (*ed.*), *Marxism and Art*, Harvester Press, Hassocks 1980.

5

less, faced with the cynicism of liberal culture and the widespread refusal in contemporary left culture to imagine the future, we would do well to look at the utopian impulse however and wherever it occurs in popular culture.

The particular form *Coronation Street*'s representation of women and the working class takes comes out of a particular historical moment, but the very fact of representing them at all is already of great interest in the wider context of media representation. The problems of representation have become an increasing focus of attention in recent years. The word representation itself allows of several different usages all of which are in play in current discussions. Thus representation may mean the re-presenting – the presenting over again – of reality, or it may be presenting-as, making reality out to be such-and-such. In the first definition, reality is taken as being unproblematically known, whereas the second definition stresses the construction of a sense or image of reality whose relation to reality itself is always problematic. Again, representation also carries the connotations of representative, typical, and at the same time representing, standing or speaking for, as in the metaphor of the MP representing her or his constituency. How a group is spoken for, or speaks for itself (and the distinction can be crucial), is how it is constituted politically, that is, in relation to power in society. In media studies, much attention has been focused on the political value of particular representations or sets of representations (Pines, 1975; Dyer, 1977; Cook and Lewington, 1979), but there has also been a much wider concern with the processes of representation in general. The debate has most consistently been posed in terms of various sorts of realist position versus various sorts of conventionalist position.* This opposition is most clearly articulated in the difference between 're-presenting reality' and 'presenting reality as' outlined above. A realist position, in its least reflexive form, would argue that the means of representation are only means for conveying 'reality', a known quantity. A conventionalist position, at its most solipsistic, would argue that 'reality' is unknowable (and perhaps non-existent) and that all representation is concerned to construct images of reality which are – in reality, as it were – *only* images.

What is significant about the essays in this book is the degree to which they are all concerned to locate *both* realist and conventionalist impulses in *Coronation Street* and soap opera. All the writers seem close to operating with a notion that reality is indeed only knowable through representations (here meaning ways of making sense) but that to say that is not the same thing as saying that representations fabricate reality. We may only see reality through glasses, and distorting ones at that, but that doesn't mean that we don't see reality.

This might be taken as the limit position of the essays. Marion Jordan and Richard Paterson seem closer to a position that sees both realism and

---

* For further discussion, see Terry Lovell, *Pictures of Reality*, 1980.

6

conventionalism (for Jordan the wit and camp, for Paterson the constraints of marketing through formulae) as formal constructions, whereas Christine Geraghty and Terry Lovell seem to retain notions of a level of relatively unmediated experience of reality (in Geraghty the sense of real time, in Lovell aspects of feeling and 'good sense'). All are tackling the question of the inter-relationship between the representation of reality and that reality of which it is a representation (see Harvey, 1978).

All are concerned too with the pleasure such representation may afford. As the debate was traditionally set up (Lowenthal, 1961), realism and pleasure were seen as antithetical. If a thing were truly realistic, it could not possibly be pleasurable, either because reality was itself unpleasant or because realism implies a stoic, or at least serious, gaze at reality. There is something of this tension to be felt in most of these essays. *Coronation Street* is seen to have set out to be realistic *but* got side-tracked into formulae and theatricality; *Coronation Street* seen to depict reality with some accuracy *but* also to be pleasurable. Yet these essays do also begin to pick their way past this tired and tiresome opposition. Once again a slight divergence between more 'realist' and more 'conventionalist' approaches (but by no means absolutely either of these positions) seems to operate. Terry Lovell's suggestion that the recognition of reality, or the confirmation of particular constructions of reality, may itself be pleasurable, offers a rapprochement between a relatively realist position on representation and the question of pleasure. Her emphasis is different from the general attack on the pleasures of recognition that certain theorists maintain,* since she is arguing that, in *Coronation Street* and soap opera, constructions of reality *other than* those serving the interests of the bourgeoisie and men may be given some recognition, and hence a certain validation and confirmation. Marion Jordan's essay comes at the question from the other (conventionalist) side, by suggesting that the wit of the series effectively foregrounds the serial's patina of realism, so that we then get pleasure from seeing how this realism is put together. Interestingly, Marion Jordan's essay also goes against theories that would propose, in a misreading of Brecht, that foregrounding devices are necessarily 'progressive'. She argues that such devices are not the preserve of a radical minority, but are widely understood and enjoyed. Audiences may be fully aware of how the media construct reality without thereby being particularly concerned to change the dominant definitions of reality enshrined in those constructions. (This observation is borne out by the work of David Morley on television audiences, 1980.)

What is surprising – and perhaps in itself rather pleasurable – is the degree to which traditional, indeed even classical, notions of aesthetic pleasure also inform most of the essays. Christine Geraghty's analysis of the formal properties of *Coronation Street* and soap opera repeatedly returns to

* The best-known statement of this position is by Colin MacCabe, 'The Classic Realist Text', in Williams, 1980.

7

notions of balance, repetition and variation that are the very core of classical aesthetics, and of Horace in particular. Though other writers identify different elements that are in play in the serials, the sense of a formal aesthetic play is present in all the essays. Indeed, the very question of the relationship between realist and conventionalist aspects of the serials does itself have this aesthetic dimension, as if the balance that plays together variation and repetition on realism and convention itself constitutes the pleasing core of the series. At times, we seem to be in a discourse more familiar from Renaissance or Enlightenment writings, or else art theory derived from Gestalt psychology (such as the work of Suzanne K. Langer, 1953), than those media studies discourses that most evidently characterise the book. Classical and Gestalt discourses propose patterns of pleasure that are not historically specific but virtually universal aspects of human culture. A polemic around this position and against Marxist aesthetic reductionism has recently been mounted by Peter Fuller (1980), and a theoretical justification from within a materialist conception of history was provided several years ago by Sebastiano Timpanaro (1976). Although not tackled head-on in these essays, support for such a position could be found here. It is a welcome position, since a hard-line relativistic position on aesthetic pleasure leaves a lot of questions unanswerable, but it is a position that needs very careful handling if we are not to fall back into assuming that what seems unchangeable is in fact unchangeable rather than the product of historical human practice.

The debates in which these papers are situated have often been conducted in unhelpfully acrimonious ways. A terroristic theoreticism has often been met by a clodhopping empiricism, with neither side listening to the other. These papers suggest that perhaps both sides have something to learn from the other, not in a spirit of liberal niceness, but rather in recognition of the seriousness of what is at stake in the debates, a seriousness the rich connotative range of the word 'representation' forces on our attention. The issue – of the politics of the representation of class and gender – has to be tackled through the seemingly less direct topics addressed in these essays. Discussion of media representation has to include the rigorous attention to form that Christine Geraghty evinces and the careful examination of conditions of production that Richard Paterson presents; it must be informed by the wider theoretical issues that Terry Lovell deals with as well as by the kind of inwardness with the aesthetic workings of the material that Marion Jordan's essay draws on. (It also requires the kind of historicisation that I have, only sketchily, pointed to above in my discussion of the moment of *The Uses of Literacy*.) The political seriousness of the endeavour is to be judged by the seriousness with which these aspects are pursued and not by tub thumping declarations of the writers' political credentials, for only this kind of intellectual seriousness will give us a real purchase on the issues and phenomena at stake.

8

CHRISTINE GERAGHTY

The Continuous Serial – A Definition

The purpose of this essay is to define the continuous serial so that *Coronation Street* can be seen not as a unique object for study but placed within the context of serials broadcast on British television and radio.* The definition I will give is not to be found in the subject matter of the serials concerned but in the way in which narrative, character and the passage of time are organised. In the first section of the piece three key characteristics will be identified, which I will argue are essential to any continuous serial. The two middle sections will analyse how narrative and characterisation are typically handled in the serial. The final section examines the way in which gossip, often seen as a distinctive feature of *Coronation Street*, is used to bind together the serial and to draw the audience into it. I hope to show how the continuous serial is able to run for years, preserving a basic stability while making enough changes to prevent tedious repetition. In their article on *World in Action*, Heath and Skirrow write that:

> the central fact of television experience is much less flow than flow and regularity; the anachronistic succession is also a constant repetition and these terms of movement and stasis can be found as well within the single programme as within the evening's viewing (Heath and Skirrow, 1977, p. 15).

This notion of movement and stasis within a programme seems a fruitful one for the study of the serial; the intention of this essay is to examine how such a process can be seen to be at work.

THE CHARACTERISTICS OF THE CONTINUOUS SERIAL

The Organisation of Time
It can be argued that the most important influence on how the audience perceives the continuous serial is its regular appearance, in the same slot every week of the year. Twice a week, three times a week, five times a week,

---

* This essay is concerned only with British television and radio serials and is not intended to cover American serials. Examples are mainly taken from four serials which were running at the time of writing – Granada's *Coronation Street*, ATV's *Crossroads* (then running four nights a week in the London area), *The Archers* and *Waggoner's Walk*, both on BBC Radio with a 15-minute episode every weekday.

the familiar signature tune alerts us to the fact that the serial is about to begin. It does not disappear 'until the autumn' or 'until the next series'. It appears every week and the time which passes between each episode is always known to the audience. Because of this, the question of how time passes in a serial, of how time is constructed and perceived by the audience, is important in distinguishing the continuous serial from the series. The series, although it also uses the same characters across a number of episodes, normally deals with a particular story within a discrete episode. One can watch *Hazell* or *Z Cars* without it mattering how much time has narratively passed between episodes. Significantly, *The Archers,* on the other hand, is announced as 'the *everyday* story of country folk' even though it is only every week day. There is an appeal here to the audience's experience of time in the real world, as if we get through our own personal events during a day and then tune in to discover what has happened in Ambridge that day.

This feeling is usefully described, in terms of the novel, by Carl Grabo as being the convention of 'unchronicled growth'. 'In the novel,' he argues, 'when the story shifts from one sub-plot to another, the characters abandoned pursue an unrecorded existence' (Grabo, 1978, p. 67). The characters in a serial, when abandoned at the end of an episode, pursue an 'unrecorded existence' until the next one begins. In other words, we are aware that day-to-day life has continued in our absence even though the problem we left at the end of the previous episode has still to be resolved. I shall discuss this development of the conventional serial cliffhanger in the section on narrative, but for the moment it is important to note that the promise – 'continued tomorrow/on Wednesday/next week' – is almost invariably not fulfilled by the serials I am discussing, as it was by the movie serial or is still by the next segment of a comic or magazine plot.

In addition, the broadcast serial, whether it be daily or weekly, appears to have gone through a similar period of time as its audience, whereas in a series, narrative time within the episode is the only criterion for time passing. Serials vary, of course, in how scrupulously they adhere to this convention of time apparently passing at the same rate as in the outside world. In *Waggoner's Walk*, a Sunday in the serial may occur on a Wednesday, but even here the sense of a day gone by between episodes is still strong. *The Archers*, on the other hand, is the most punctilious in paralleling real time (7.05 p.m. transmission) so that if a character says that it is Thursday it is usually Thursday in the outside world. Even *The Archers,* though, cannot stick to this rigidly and events occurring at the weekend, for instance, have to be broadcast on a Friday or a Monday. *Coronation Street* also gives the impression of leaving a literal time between episodes, and significant days in the outside world such as bank holidays or special anniversaries are referred to and celebrated on the right day. In both *The Archers* and *Coronation Street*, public events – the Silver Jubilee, the decimilisation of the coinage, or the Royal Show in *The Archers* – are discussed in the programme as they are occurring in the outside world.

The strength of this convention can be illustrated by what happens when it is broken. When a lorry crashed into the 'Rovers Return' in *Coronation Street* in 1979, the dramatic nature of the incident was underlined by the spinning out of time. Two or three hours of narrative time dealing with the clearing of rubble and the discovery of victims took days and weeks of real time: tension was emphasised in this way and the normal feeling of day-to-day life was gone.

The Sense of a Future
The second characteristic of the continuous serial is the sense of a future, the continual postponement of the final resolution. Unlike the series which is advertised as having a specific number of episodes, the serial is endless. The apparent multifariousness of the plots, their inextricability from each other, the everyday quality of narrative time and events, all encourage us to believe that this is a narrative whose future is not yet written. Even events which would offer a suitable ending in other narrative forms are never a final ending in the continuous serial: a wedding is not a happy ending but opens up the possibilities of stories about married life and divorce; a character's departure from a serial does not mean that s/he will not turn up again several years later, as Lillian Bellamy does in *The Archers*. It is perhaps this sense of a future which also explains the way in which deaths in serials (Grace Archer, Martha Longhurst in *Coronation Street*, Amy Turtle in *Crossroads*) remain as high spots, remembered and indeed mysticised, not so much because of the characters involved, but because they are the only moments which are irreversible. Ray Langton in *Coronation Street*, paralysed from the waist down in a coach crash, regained the use of his legs within five months, but not even the scriptwriters can bring Ernie Bishop back to life.

The impossibility of 'closing' a serial was illustrated by events in *Waggoner's Walk*, which was brought to an untimely end by BBC cuts in May/June 1980. Very little attempt was made to tie up loose ends and several stories were abandoned *in medias res*. Indeed, the writers seem to have humorously recognised that a serial – even in this situation – has a future, by finishing the serial with a proposal of marriage which the woman concerned asks for time to think about. 'Of course,' comes the reply, 'you have all the time in the world', and it is left to the signature tune to bring the serial to an end. One is left with a sense that the serial has not stopped but is still taking place, an extreme case of 'unchronicled growth'.

The Interweaving of Stories
The third characteristic of a continuous serial is the way in which two or three stories are woven together and presented to the audience over a number of episodes. It is interesting to compare this with how stories are handled in series. In series such as *Hazell* or *Sergeant Cribb*, the story, as I have pointed out, is usually resolved within a single episode. Other series such as *The Brothers* or *Fox*, which are in effect non-continuous serials, do

have several storylines, but usually only one is dealt with at any length in a specific episode although the others may appear as sub-plots to keep them ticking over. It is characteristic of the continuous serial, however, that two or three stories dealt with are given approximately equal time in each episode and very often reflect on and play off each other. As one story finishes, another is begun so that at least two stories are always in progress. Looking at an episode from *Coronation Street* (29.12.76) may help to illustrate how this works.

The episode is concerned mainly with two stories. In one, Annie Walker is waiting anxiously for the result of a breathalyser test; in the second, Bet Lynch, who has moved in as 'housekeeper' to Mike Baldwin, is preparing for a party she is giving in his house. Both stories are worked through in separate scenes; both are discussed by non-participants in the pub; thematically, both deal with the common-sense notion of 'pride coming before a fall'. Annie's pride in her car and her respectability is being dented by the humiliation of the breath test and its aftermath, while Bet's pride in the house and her new relationship with Baldwin presages, for those who know *Coronation Street*, a certain fall. During the episode, Annie's story is resolved when she learns that the test has proved negative, and a new story is introduced, at the end of the episode, when Len Fairclough reveals at the party that he has had a letter from his son. Thus, the episode starts with two stories but when one is brought to an end, another immediately begins. It should also be noted that, although this particular tale of Annie and her car is resolved, Annie's pride still remains as a potential source for similar stories. It is possible for a serial to cover a wide range of stories and styles without disturbing the serial format by playing them against very familiar elements – the signature tune, the setting, long-standing characters. The audience is presented with a rich pattern of incident and characterisation – the dramatic is mixed in with the everyday, the tragic with the comic, the romantic with the mundane. The proportions will vary from serial to serial. *The Archers* sometimes seems to consist of nothing but the humdrum, while *Crossroads* frequently veers towards melodrama. In *Coronation Street*, comic stories centring on the Ogdens or Eddie Yeats often run alongside the more 'serious' dramatic stories. But because the unfamiliar is introduced within a context of the very familiar, the audience is able to cope with enormous shifts in style and material, even within one episode, which might otherwise be expected to occur across a whole evening's viewing.

These three characteristics, then, are the essential elements of the continuous serial and they distinguish it from other forms such as the series or the dramatisation of a novel. It is clear that all three – the organisation of time, the sense of an unwritten future, the interweaving of plots – are closely tied in with how narrative is handled in the serial. The next section therefore takes up the issue of narrative more directly.

Much of the research done on narrative has concentrated on works which are read with the knowledge that they will come to an end. Narrative organisation is described as functioning through tension and the resolution of that tension by reaching a satisfactory ending (Scholes and Kellogg, 1979, p. 212). Todorov describes 'a minimum narrative . . . without which we cannot say that there is any narrative at all' as 'a movement between equilibriums which are similar but not identical' (Todorov, 1975, p. 163). The narrative ends, in other words, with the establishment of an equilibrium which balances that which was disturbed or disrupted at the beginning of the text. Barthes' work in *S/Z* has alerted us to the way in which narratives work by posing enigmas and questions which draw the reader through the text in search of an answer. The reader is kept involved through this pursuit which is in fact a pursuit of resolution. In the end, after delays, confusions and red herrings, comes the final resolution when 'all enigmas are disclosed' (Barthes, 1975, p. 209). Drawing on such sources, some critical writing has described the narrative process solely in terms of closure. Gill Davies sums up this position concisely in her article 'Teaching about Narrative':

> Narrative in both the novel and the film has the same effect. It creates a sense of inevitability and closure in the action is felt to be predestined, tidy and without contradiction (Davies, 1978-9, p. 59).

In the same article, she writes that narrative is precipitated by an initial problem which it is the work of the text to render harmless and resolve:

> no new issues are raised, everything is resolved and the audience is presented with a closed and comforting symmetry. (ibid.)

In the light of this emphasis on resolution and closure, work on serials and narrative offers a new perspective. As I have shown, serials are marked by their sense of the future, the promise which they hold out of being endless. While individual stories are resolved, the continuous serial must go on and the audience must be kept involved. In this section, therefore, I want to look at narrative in continuous serials in the light of their endlessness and, in particular, to concentrate on two devices of key importance – the use of the cliffhanger and of moments of temporary resolution. In addition, I will examine how the serial sets up different narrative conventions from those of the book and film and how this difference affects the audience's engagement with a continually unfinished text.

The Cliffhanger

The cliffhanger is often seen as the traditional hallmark of the serial. In this section, therefore, I want to look at how the use of the cliffhanger formally differentiates the serial from the complete novel or film and at how the serials I am discussing have adapted this device.

All fictional – and indeed non-fictional – forms attempt to engage the audience by the posing and working through of an enigma. The importance of this strategy varies, however, from genre to genre. On the one hand there is the classic 30s detective novel in which the puzzle is all, outstanding character traits (violent temper, apparent timidity) only serving as clues or red herrings in the solution to the conundrum; on the other hand, there are novels like *A Portrait of a Lady* or *Mrs Dalloway* in which the evocation of character and setting is of far greater importance than the unravelling of the plot. In all cases, however, the resolution of the narrative is contained within the text. If we want to know what happens in a novel, we can read it all in one sitting, turn to the end of the book or dip into it at random. We can (at least in most local cinemas) choose to see the end of a film first – which is why Hitchcock's films were often advertised specifically with the notice, 'No one allowed to enter in the last ten minutes.' To some extent the spectator/ reader can control his/her relationship to the suspense in these cases, while accepting that s/he must not break the rules if a specific form of enjoyment is to be gained. But the suspense in serials is forced on us, so that we are left waiting between one episode and the next, literally in suspense. The cliff-hanger marks this enforced interruption.

The cliffhanger is normally thought of in terms of silent movie serials. The unfolding of the action is cut off at a crucial point so that the enigma is unresolved and the leading characters remain in danger. The audience is left with questions – how will the heroine escape, can the hero out-manoeuvre the enemy? The tension which arises from the sudden break in the narrative is expressed by the cliffhanger so that the different directions which the story could take are frozen until the next episode. The serials I am writing about, however, only occasionally use the cliffhanger device with its original dramatic effect. It is important to note the narrative construction through which this shift has been achieved. Continuing problems run through every serial, which the audience can follow while missing specific episodes. In *Coronation Street*, one such story would be the question of Deirdre's new relationships after the break-up of her marriage; similarly, in *The Archers*, several years ago, questions hung for a long time over the future of Jennifer Archer's marital status; in *Crossroads*, recurringly, there is a threat to Meg Richardson's control over the motel and she has to fight to retain it. These overall stories contribute to the framework of the serial, within which each episode will have its own structure, working with two or more plots, of which one is often used as comic balance to a more serious drama. The weighting of this interweaving will vary from serial to serial – *Coronation Street* and *Emmerdale Farm* rely more on the comic/serious balance than does *Crossroads*. In all serials, though, this episodic construction means that while major overall questions are left unanswered and unresolved, the cliffhanger can emanate from some minor matter, often comically pre-

14

sented and easily forgotten. It is, therefore, merely a formal device and is not necessarily related to the potential outcome of the story. In other words, it is a cliffhanger almost because it occurs at the end of an episode, and cuts us off from the created world of the serial. Because of this, the cliffhanger, although frequently used in the serial to pose a question, varies in intensity and importance. It is not necessary therefore to produce moments of high drama at the end of *every* episode, and a potentially rigid device is made more flexible by using it comically or for minor events. In terms of the balance between repetition (the regular use of a cliffhanger) and variation within the programmes, this is an important difference between the current television and radio serials and the much more rigid movie serials.

There is one further variant in how the cliffhanger is used to engage the audience with the narrative of the serial. This depends on the type of knowledge the audience is given within a specific episode and which in turn affects the kind of puzzle which is offered to the listener/viewer. Audiences can be kept in the dark over a particular problem – Benny, in *Crossroads*, is accused of murder, we do not know whether he did it or not, we want to get an answer to this question. Or the audience can be given knowledge – Benny is accused of a murder which we see that he did not commit; how can this mistake be remedied? These are two different types of suspense, the former much more a question of solving the mystery, the latter encouraging our involvement with a character. It is interesting to note here that *Coronation Street* uses the latter form of suspense much more frequently, but all serials use both these variants, teasing the audience with limited and carefully structured knowledge.

Moments of Temporary Resolution
It is clear then that the cliffhanger is an important device in the narrative organisation of the continuous serial. Its use, however, is also balanced by the rarer moments of resolution in the serial, the points at which a new harmony is very temporarily reached. Serials vary in how much they use this strategy. *The Archers* quite often finishes, particularly at the end of the week, with the coming together of the family at a meal or a gathering. The other serials tend to save such moments for festivals such as Christmas or communal occasions like weddings or funerals. Such moments are marked by the suppression of other stories, even though they will be picked up in the next episode. For once, the harmony within the group of characters will be stressed so that quarrels and differences which would threaten the equilibrium are temporarily suspended. The final image of such an episode is not one which looks forward to the next instalment but one which rounds off this one – the bridal pair embracing, a toast at a family celebration, a group of characters at the end of a street party. Of course, there is never a final resolution since the audience is aware of stories which are to be continued, but such moments do provide a respite from the hermeneutic dramas of the cliffhanger. Indeed, the two alternatives, the temporary resolution and the

cliffhanger, work together to provide variations within the established pattern of the serials' organisation.

The Use of the Past
So far, in this section on narrative, I have discussed how the serial form plays on the audience's desire to know what happens next. It is clear that the audience's engagement is also with what has happened in the past. The serial offers, as we have seen, an attenuated narrative which may in the case of successful serials go on for twenty or thirty years. In this situation, all viewers/listeners do not have the same knowledge of the serial's past and events remembered vividly by some are unknown to others. Episodes may have been missed; the viewers/listeners may be comparative newcomers to the programme; they may see/hear only a limited number of episodes, perhaps because of regular commitments elsewhere. Little attempt is made to bring the audience up-to-date with events it may have missed and the announcers who introduce the programmes obviously cannot offer a résumé of what has happened so far. There is therefore no guarantee that individual members of the audience will know very much about a particular serial's history.

It should be noted, however, that some viewers/listeners do remember a serial's past very clearly and expect any references to it to be accurate, down to the last detail. This accumulation of knowledge by the committed audience is recognised by those working on the programmes, who boast about the detailed attention to minutiae which their audience give the serial. The *Coronation Street* production team includes a programme historian who ensures that any references to the past are correct. Knowledge gained from watching or listening to the programme can be reinforced by reading the books based on the serials or magazines produced to mark special events. *Coronation Street*'s 2,000th episode, for instance, was celebrated with a 'souvenir album' which included the script of the first episode and a history of events in the Street over the last twenty years. The serial, therefore, operates in a situation in which it must be accessible to all viewers while, at the same time, be accurate about its own accumulated past. This double necessity has certain effects on both the narrative in serials and the audience's involvement in that process.

Conversation in serials seldom turns to past events and it is very rare for a plot to hinge on or be affected by what has happened in even the recent past. There are set pieces when Ena Sharples talks about her girlhood or characters in *Emmerdale Farm* reminisce about the old life in the Dales, but such references draw on nostalgia for a community experience rather than knowledge of events in the serial's own history. Television serials can sometimes hint at the importance of a character who has appeared earlier in the serial by using his/her photograph in the décor. Thus, the photograph of the deceased Jack Walker is prominent in Annie's living room and is sometimes specifically focused on in her times of crisis. However, if knowledge of the past is crucial to the audience's understanding of the plot, this is usually worked directly into the drama. One example of how this is done can be seen in the way in which the 25th anniversary of Grace Archer's death was handled in *The Archers*. First, Phil, who was her husband, is heard to be brusque with his son David, and generally upset for no reason; a conversation with his current wife, Jill, lets the audience know about the anniversary but does not give us any details; finally, Tom Forrest tells David the full story of the fire and Grace's death. Thus David, a member of the younger generation, stands in for those in the audience who are ignorant of what has happened and without disturbing the narrative flow allows them to be filled in on a piece of Archer history.

This example is particularly interesting because to *aficionados* of *The Archers* an explanation of such a famous event was unnecessary and indeed there were complaints that Tom had got the details wrong. I want to discuss later the audience's relationship with the serial form, but I think it is worth mentioning here the way in which the regular viewer/listener can fill out the narrative with recollections of past events in a way which is more significant than mere attention to historical detail would suggest. Thus, although references to Bet Lynch's illegitimate child are rare, a viewer who remembers the fact can bring its resonances to Bet's subsequent stories. Any viewer will recognise that Betty Turpin is a kindly, indeed motherly character, but if one remembers that she has had a son who was brought up by her sister then her behaviour has a sad edge of frustration. It is also possible for a viewer/listener to raise questions within the narrative which may not in fact be answered since they are not on the scriptwriter's agenda. Thus, while listening to a discussion of the problems of tenant farmers in *The Archers*, it is possible to speculate on the eventual return of Lillian Bellamy (the landlady) from Guernsey without even hearing her name mentioned. I would not want to overstress this contribution of the audience to the narrative process since clearly it is limited by the serial's own parameters. Nevertheless, it seems to me that the kind of work the audience can do has greater potential in the serial than in other narrative forms.

I have said that the people involved in producing serials pride themselves on being accurate about details of a serial's past; we have also seen that they cannot *assume* knowledge on the audience's part and therefore do not often refer to the past. This means in effect that serials actually provide more room to move within plots – though not within the established world of the serial – than series or plays where the action takes place in a single broadcast. For example, characters can disappear with vague explanations of holidays or visits to relatives or even no explanation at all. Strands of the plot which are not cleared up are lost in the establishment of the next stories, and any puzzled viewer/listener wonders if s/he missed an episode or two. Thus one week Sandy Richardson in *Crossroads* is being begged to return from London for the sake of the motel; the next week he (and everyone else) talks about his return as being caused by his failure in London. The two explanations are not put together as a complex whole; they are used as mutually exclusive motivations – one working for last week's stories, the other offering possibilities for this week. *Crossroads*, in fact, uses this device of jumping across lacunae in the narrative by turning the audience's attention elsewhere more frequently than most serials, but it is used by them all.

Although the accumulated past is important to a serial, one could also say that the ability to 'forget' what has happened in the serial's past is equally crucial. If the serial had to carry the heavy weight of its own past it would not be able to carry on. The stories would grind to a halt while the implications of past events were explained to new viewers/listeners. Instead, the serials, while clearly accepting, as in the case of Grace Archer's death, that they have a past, cannot be bound by it. A rigid adherence to their own history is rejected in favour of a more flexible approach which allows serials to function in the present.

In this section, I have stressed the way in which the formal narrative strategies of the serial differ from those of the complete film or episode in a series and I have examined the use of the cliffhanger and the serial's past. These strategies are important because they allow the serial, while always operating within the familiar format, to provide sufficient variation to prevent a sense of complete repetition. Thus, the past can be actively used within a story, be fleetingly referred to, or remain a potential resource for the audience. The serial may break at a point of unfinished action or high tension, at moments of no particular dramatic importance or at moments of temporary resolution. These variations are limited but they are sufficient to give 'movement' and difference within the repetition described by Heath and Skirrow. The rest of this essay will show that this use of narrative strategies based on difference and repetition is backed up by similar variations at the level of characterisation and plot.

CHARACTERISATION AND PLOT

In this section, I want to study the way in which characterisation and plot in a serial interlock in a way which provides a familiar base for the viewer but which generates enough surprises to prevent tedium. Thus the same plots can be used again with different inflections, the same character can be used in various ways, new characters can be introduced and disappear without comment, the same situation can generate different expectations. We can see how this process works by looking first at how the characters in a serial are used and secondly at how they are placed within particular plots.

The Use of Characters

A serial always uses more characters than a play or even a series in order to give variety and so that characters do not get 'used up' too quickly. Although based on one community (the Street, Ambridge, Emmerdale), a serial will have a fairly wide variation among the characters in terms of age, relation-

18

ships, and attitudes because, as we shall see, such variations permit a wider range of stories. A serial must have a core of characters who appear regularly over the years and who become familiar to the consistent viewer/listener. In addition, most serials introduce new characters for a small number of episodes featuring stories perhaps not applicable to the main characters.

Because the serial has to be comprehensible to both the committed follower and the casual viewer, and given the number of characters involved, characterisation has to be swift and sharp; the immediate sense of what a character is and what role s/he is likely to play has to be given quickly, using such elements as clothes and voice. The different styles of dress adopted by Hilda Ogden, Elsie Tanner and Annie Walker in *Coronation Street* tell us immediately the kind of characters we are engaged with. The much imitated voice of Walter Gabriel in *The Archers* gives us a clear idea of his age, social position and the fact that he is a comic character, before he has even finished a sentence. It should be noted, and this will be taken up later, that the referral point for these judgments is more often within the serial than out in the real world. Thus, it is precisely the contrast of appearance which is important – Hilda's rollers compared with Elsie's hair-*do* and Annie's hair *style*, her apron with Elsie's ruffled blouses and Annie's 'afternoon' dresses. We can only place Walter Gabriel's voice so exactly by referring not to our scanty knowledge of rural dialects but to the other voices in *The Archers* – Phil's modulated tones, Jack Woolley's hectoring, *nouveau riche* style, Dan Archer's less comic version of the dialect. In both cases, it is the fitting of a characteristic into the scale provided by the serial which enables us to place a character.

Having commented on this mode of characterisation, I want to group the characters in serials in three ways which I will argue provide the base for their use within the narrative. One can see each character as an individuated character, as a serial type and as the holder of a position, distinctions which will become clear in the following comments.

The *individuated character* is the character marked by traits which are presented as uniquely his or her own. (It is this aspect which is emphasised by articles in the press.) Certain characters, very often but not always those used for comic effect, will be particularly marked by one such trait – Albert Tatlock's stinginess, Joe Grundy's grouchy unsociability, Clarrie Larkin's naïvety (in *The Archers*). Others, especially the longstanding characters, will be constructed out of a number of such traits. Thus, Hilda Ogden is presented as a nag, a gossip and a woman who can occasionally take on a real dignity when confronted with her lot; David Hunter (*Crossroads*) is built up as a man with a smooth, suave exterior which conceals a capacity for feeling real hurt. It is by emphasising the number of these individuated characters that the serial is able to reinforce the notion that it is giving us an endlessly rich pattern of life and people.

The second way of looking at these characters is by seeing them as *serial types*. I have mentioned before that our reference point for understanding a character is very often within the serial rather than outside it. It seems to me also that certain characters become types within whose range of traits other characters are also then shaped. Thus there is an 'Elsie Tanner type' – sexy, rather tartily dressed, hot-tempered, impulsive – who is also recognisable in other women in *Coronation Street* – Rita, Suzie, Bet (and I would also include Len Fairclough as a male equivalent). In addition, other women in the serial are defined by specifically *not* being an 'Elsie Tanner type' – Mavis, Emily and Gail, who has graduated from apprenticeship in this type to being its opposite. Similarly, in *The Archers*, there are a number of women – Jill, Carol, Peggy, Christine – who are basically the same type. They have different individuated characteristics – Jill's supposedly left-wing views, Carol's business efficiency – but they are all middle-aged, middle-class, concerned, caring women. And in *Crossroads* it is possible to pick out the 'Meg Richardson type' – Meg herself, Tish Hope, Meg's daughter Jill, Rosemary Hunter (before her breakdown) – who are all characterised by a combination of impeccable grooming, a hard exterior and an inward relish of emotion.

The third way of grouping the same set of characters is as *holders of a status position*: by this, I am referring to the position they occupy in the serial in terms crucially of sex, age and marital position and sometimes in terms of class and work. Thus, in *Coronation Street*, Ken Barlow, Steve Fisher, Mike Baldwin, Eddie Yeats, Fred Gee and even Albert Tatlock, however different they may be as individuated characters and serial types, are all, at the time of writing, unmarried men and therefore available for stories centring on courtship and marriage. The death of Renee has returned Alf Roberts to that position while Len Fairclough and Brian Tilsley have moved out of it by actually getting married. Other serials, *Waggoner's Walk* for example, use a number of characters who are both career women and mothers; *The Archers*, a number of male farmers; *Crossroads*, a number of unattached women, including Meg who is always being returned to that position. Of course, characters may hold more than one position, depending on what is being emphasised. Thus Tony Archer is a husband, son and father as well as being a farmer, and the emphasis will clearly depend on the particular story he is involved in at a given moment.

It is important perhaps to stress that these three categories are not exclusive; all characters at all times can be seen as an individuated character, a serial type and the holder of a particular status position. It is the interaction of the three categories which allows the character to be used in different ways and which gives both stability and flexibility to the narrative.

Characters in the Narrative

This analysis of the serial characters makes it possible to see how they can be used within the narrative organisation of the serial. It is clear that while some plots are available to everyone, others will be limited to those of a particular type or status position. Big events – birth, marriage, death – are used sparingly to give them the feeling of a special occasion. (The complications of several characters dying and/or marrying at the same time could render *Coronation Street* something of a *Soap*-like farce.) Plots centring on marriage or birth are available to a limited, though still wide, range of characters; that of death is available to all, but different character traits will give the event its particular feeling of poignancy, grief, shock or even relief. When such events happen, they tend to take up a lot of time within an episode and, particularly in the case of television serials, are supported by off-screen coverage such as the production of special magazines.*

General plots, on the other hand, are the staple of the serial, the basis of the output. They revolve – in the serials I am discussing – around problems of relationships such as arise within marriages, between generations, in friendships and through quarrels and difficulties at home. These general plots are available to all characters since everyone is involved, in one way or another, in this complex web of relationships. Variety is then available through the individuals involved, which makes for the difference between, for instance, the same story concerning Annie and Billy Walker, Ivy and Brian Tilsley or Gail and her mother. We scarcely notice that the stories are centred around the same pressures between parent and child unless a play on that similarity specifically draws it to our attention. The serial type and status position of a character will indicate whether s/he is suitable for a particular story dealing with a particular relationship. Thus, if a plot in *Coronation Street* is to centre on a spectacular set piece of a quarrel it is likely to involve an 'Elsie Tanner type' who is the kind of character to indulge in and probably enjoy a major row. It is important to note, though, that it is possible to add a further element of variety by surprising the audience with a change in position or a character acting against type. Thus, the revelation that Bet Lynch was a mother put her in a position unknown to and unexpected by the audience. The use of characters against type, rather than status position, is more common and very effective. Emily Bishop's anger, when expressed, is more surprising and moving than Elsie Tanner's simply because it comes from an unexpected source. In *The Archers*, Joe Grundy's moments of compassion after Doris Archer's death have the same ability momentarily to surprise the audience.

Specific plots, unlike big events and general plots, are much more rigid in their use of characters. They are not available to everyone but are limited to those with certain character traits or to the holders of specific positions. Thus, in *Coronation Street*, any plot involving petty crime would almost certainly use Eddie Yeats and/or Stan Ogden (in earlier days, it would have been Dennis Tanner or Sunny Jim); in *The Archers*, it would use Joe Grundy and his sons; plots about show business, in *Coronation Street*, would involve Rita Fairclough. Very often occasional characters are brought in for these specific plots – the manager of Rita's nightclub, for instance, or a visiting

---

* Rita and Len's wedding, for instance, was marked by the production of a special magazine.

union official or 'agitator' for stories about the factory in *Coronation Street*. Such additional characters both give variety and increase the number and range of specific plots available.

Two Weddings

The variety which is achieved by this interaction can be mapped out by looking at two examples of the same 'big event' plot in *Coronation Street* – the wedding of Rita Littlewood and Len Fairclough and that of Emily Bishop and Arnold Swain. I have used the diagram form to show more concisely the implications of the two events (see Fig. 1).

The diagrams show that the same story holds quite different resonances and potential for future developments. The diagram for Rita and Len's wedding shows that the potential for general plots is likely to come from the clash of similar types and that specific plots will be available, centring on Rita's nightclub job and the fact that they have an employer/employee as well as a husband/wife relationship. The second wedding, on the other hand, shows the possibility of general plots which arise from the audience's uncertainty over Arnold, a relative newcomer, as the holder of a position and a serial type. Nevertheless, we know that the bullying which is an individuated characteristic of Arnold will fit in with the passivity and suffering which mark Emily as a serial type and that a point can be reached at which she will fight back. Thus, the same big event plot, by using different characters, creates different situations and generates a variety of possibilities for future action.

The ways in which individuated character/serial type/position holder fit into the big event/general plot/specific plot seem endless. It is important to note that what this interaction is designed to do is precisely to seem endless. One story can be repeated with different characters every few years; one character will disappear to be replaced by one of the same type and different position or same position and different type. The solid base of general plots, serial types and the more or less constant set of status positions remains while the specific plots and individuated characteristics give us the potential of variety. Always the same, always changing – that seems to be the continual dynamic of the serial and the essence of its use of character in the narrative.

THE ROLE OF GOSSIP IN THE SERIAL

Gossip within the Serial

In this final section, I want to try to analyse the role of gossip, which is frequently seen as being a characteristic of the serial and is quite often commented on within the serials themselves. On one level, gossip helps to create the feeling of day-to-dayness referred to at the beginning of this piece. (No one in *The Sweeney* or *Hazell* has time for aimless speculation about the doings of their neighbours.) More importantly, gossip in the serial constitutes a commentary on the action.

Fig. 1

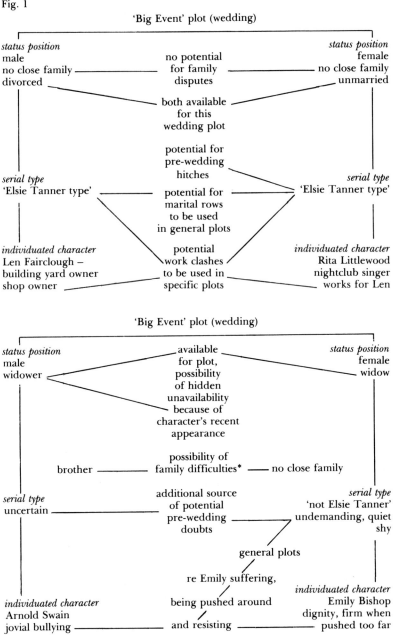

'Big Event' plot (wedding)

| status position
male
no close family
divorced | no potential
for family
disputes | status position
female
no close family
unmarried |

both available
for this
wedding plot

potential for
pre-wedding
hitches

| serial type
'Elsie Tanner type' | potential for
marital rows
to be used
in general plots | serial type
'Elsie Tanner type' |

| individuated character
Len Fairclough –
building yard owner
shop owner | potential
work clashes
to be used in
specific plots | individuated character
Rita Littlewood
nightclub singer
works for Len |

'Big Event' plot (wedding)

| status position
male
widower | available
for plot,
possibility
of hidden
unavailability
because of
character's recent
appearance | status position
female
widow |

brother ——— possibility of
family difficulties* ——— no close family

| serial type
uncertain | additional source
of potential
pre-wedding
doubts | serial type
'not Elsie Tanner'
undemanding, quiet
shy |

general plots
re Emily suffering,

| individuated character
Arnold Swain
jovial bullying | being pushed around
and resisting | individuated character
Emily Bishop
dignity, firm when
pushed too far |

* These diagrams were drawn before the revelation of Arnold's bigamy.

23

Much of the gossip which takes place provides the audience with new information or gives more detail about what has been happening. It plays an important role formally in binding together the various plots and the different characters and making them coherent. Thus, a character involved in one story will, in apparently casual conversation, pass on information about that story and receive, in exchange, news about the other plots in which s/he is not involved. The locations in which gossip can easily take place are therefore among the most frequently used sets in the serial – the pubs and corner shops in *Coronation Street*, *The Archers*, *Waggoner's Walk* and *Emmerdale Farm*, Coronation Street itself, the village green or the church hall in *The Archers*.* In these public locations, characters can appear and disappear, as required, in a way which seems quite natural.† The Rovers Return, for example, can present a continually shifting pattern of characters (and hence conversation) as members of one group of drinkers move to another and characters arrive and depart. A scene with two or three characters chatting about one story can wholly change direction with the arrival of another character with a different set of news. Such a setting means that the different plots can be brought together and commented on by characters who may not be directly involved in the action. This running commentary reveals the different moral positions which are taken up by the characters who comment on what is going on – Ken Barlow's liberal views counterpoint Ena's fundamentalist tenets – and provide the audience with a range of perspectives from which to understand the action. In addition, such conversations nearly always move on to speculation about what will happen next and what the characters involved are likely to do. This kind of speculative gossip both encourages the audience to pursue the enigma dangled before it and provides us with an insight into the characters concerned.

Gossip very often has a part in the action itself. Stories very frequently revolve round questions of knowledge or ignorance on the part of different characters, and the decision to tell a character about a previously unknown event is often a major issue. Such questions occur continually in the serials. In *Coronation Street*, how many people should be told about the death of Bet's son? How is Hilda Ogden to tell those who are striking on her behalf that she has got a new job? Should Deirdre Langton be told that her husband has been seen with another woman? Should Peggy Archer be told that her daughter, Lillian, has lied to her about a visit to Ambridge? Will Clarrie Larkin and the Grundys keep quiet about Nelson Gabriel's business venture? Knowledge revealed through gossip becomes, in this situation, some-

---

* It seems to me that the reason why *Crossroads* appears to lack cohesiveness and sometimes gives the impression of being a set of parallel plots is that it uses gossip as cement in this way far less often than the other serials. The motel lobby does not provide a suitable place for this kind of running commentary in the same way as a pub or corner shop elsewhere.

† Characters who would not meet at home or work can bump into each other in the pub or shop with the randomness of casual meetings in real life.

thing almost tangible, to be given, withheld, revealed accidentally or hinted at. Gossip becomes then not just a running commentary but an important part of the action, and it is almost impossible to draw the line between action and comment on that action.

Gossip outside the Serial

We have seen how gossip operates within the serial, both playing an important part at the level of action and presenting the audience with information, ideas and speculation on what might happen next. I would also argue that, in terms of information and speculation, gossip operates in a similar way outside the programmes in the discussion which a serial generates among its regular followers. The attraction of a successful serial is that it offers us a place, a metaphoric elbow on the bar, as commentator on the events as they unfold and our years of watching/listening make us experts. Such conversations will involve being filled in on recent episodes ('What happened in *Coronation Street* last night?') or on events in the distant past. They then move on to speculation so that discussion about who Deirdre Langton will eventually marry or whether Shula Archer will return from Bangkok is carried on not only by the characters in the serial but by the audience as well. This is not to say that the audience in general has been conned into thinking that the world of the serial is the real world. Indeed, the pleasure of such discussions comes from performing the delicate balancing act of discussing the characters as if they were real people with histories, motivations and futures while at the same time recognising the formal conventions of the serial in which they appear. We are told in newspaper reports, for instance, that Suzie Birchall and Steve Fisher are to be written out of *Coronation Street*. We can use this knowledge to speculate on how this will be done; will Steve be sacked, will they go off together, will Suzie make a success, this time, of things in London? It is this kind of informed speculation among the audience which characterises the response to a serial and which differentiates it from any other television form.

CONCLUSION

In this essay, I have discussed the formal terms within which a continuous serial operates and have tried to assess some of the effects of this process. The continuous serial has to work with a punishing schedule, normally appearing on television more than once a week and sometimes, on radio, five times a week. In order to do this, it establishes a base which becomes increasingly familiar to its audience while maintaining sufficient flexibility to be able to present apparently different situations. It provides us with the feeling of an unwritten future while giving necessary access to the past. We are constantly left wondering what will happen next – occasionally with a real cliffhanger. It presents us with 'new' events which are endless variations on regular patterns and provides a range of characters which is both varied

25

and limited. This balance of change and repetition is achieved through the organisation of narrative and character, and the succession of the narrative is cemented together by gossip, both inside and outside the text. I hope that this discussion of the serial in general will provide a useful base for the more specific work on *Coronation Street* which follows.

MARION JORDAN

Realism and Convention

There are obvious difficulties in treating as homogeneous a programme which has gone on the air more than 2,000 times. None the less, though viewers might well dispute endlessly as to the aesthetic merits of particular (groups of) programmes, they would all recognise any episode of *Coronation Street* as part of a continuum. And this recognisability cannot depend merely on the continuity of plot-line, or even of character, since individual viewers must be able to pick up programmes randomly and not feel lost. My aim here is to analyse the elements of this continuity, rather than to examine the varying nature of the programme in the hands of different writers and producers. Examples will, therefore, be drawn from a range of programmes, particularly from early (1960) transmissions, from the period 1974-5, and from more recent (1979) episodes.

Tony Warren, the prime mover of *Coronation Street,* describes its conception in terms which betray an essential ambivalence. The memo with which he 'sold' the programme to his supervisors represents it as a slice-of-life, even semi-documentary, presentation:

A fascinating freemasonry, a volume of unwritten rules. These are the driving forces behind life in a working-class street in the North of England. The purpose of *Florizel Street* [as it then was] is to examine a community of this nature, and in so doing to entertain. (Warren, 1969, p. 58)

At the same time, acutely conscious of himself and his attitude to work as essentially 'theatrical', he describes how, while waiting for the first screening of *Coronation Street*, he went into a church and burnt a candle: 'I am neither Roman Catholic nor given to formal religion,' he explains, 'but I had been brought up on Ivor Novello musicals, so it seemed the right thing to do' (op. cit., pp. 66–7). It is this, ostensibly incompatible, combination of a basic documentary Realism (which seeks always to disguise, even to deny, its own use of conventions) and the open, even camp, flaunting of popular art conventions in *Coronation Street* that this essay seeks to examine.

Coronation Street was first shown in 1960 at a time when the cinema, the novel, the stage, were all engaged in a conscious effort to achieve 'relevance' by treating what they regarded as the social problems of the working class in terms which were recognisable to members of that class. Social Realism became an important, perhaps dominant, mode in fiction. The very choice of the term 'Realism' has, of course, always asserted a claim that the mode is

27

closer to reality than are other forms of art, but the incompleteness of that relationship has also been acknowledged implicitly (if not always accurately) in the addition of such qualifications as 'classical', 'social', 'psychological'.

Coronation Street certainly adopted some of the conventions of Social Realism, many of which are easily adaptable to the serial form. Briefly the genre of Social Realism demands that life should be presented in the form of a narrative of personal events, each with a beginning, a middle and an end, important to the central characters concerned but affecting others in only minor ways; that though these events are ostensibly about *social* problems they should have as one of their central concerns the settling of people in life; that the resolution of these events should always be in terms of the effect of personal interventions; that characters should be either working-class or of the classes immediately visible to the working classes (shopkeepers, say, or the two-man business) and should be credibly accounted for in terms of the 'ordinariness' of their homes, families, friends; that the locale should be urban and provincial (preferably in the industrial north); that the settings should be commonplace and recognisable (the pub, the street, the factory, the home and more particularly the kitchen); that the time should be 'the present'; that the style should be such as to suggest an unmediated, unprejudiced and complete view of reality; to give, in summary, the impression that the reader, or viewer, has spent some time at the expense of the characters depicted.

Along with these conventions *Coronation Street* has accepted also some of the existing conventions of soap opera proper, notably that though events must carry their own minor conclusions they must not be seen as finally resolving; that there should be an intertwining of plots so deployed as to imply a multiplicity of experience whilst effectively covering only a narrow range of directly 'personal' events; that these personal events should be largely domestic; that there should be substantial roles for women; that all roles should involve a serious degree of stereotyping; that the most plausible setting, in view of these later requirements, would be the home; and that the long-term passage of fictional time should mirror fairly accurately the actual passage of time.

Clearly these two sets of conventions fit together neatly. The essentially individualistic genre of Social Realism, with its stress on personal events, the finding of a partner, the ignoring of a world not immediately visible to its protagonists, happily accepts soap opera's requirements for a multiplicity of plots, a lack of dramatic resolution, a setting in the home, and a prominence of stereotyped women. From the fusion of these two there emerges a specific television form that one may think of as Soap-Opera Realism. If the phrase seems irritatingly paradoxical it is perhaps fair to ask that we consider as though for the first time the phrases 'Classical Realism', 'Psychological Realism' etc. which are its precedents, since they too are, if taken literally, equally paradoxical. Other examples of the genre are to be seen in programmes like *The Liver Birds* (admittedly a series rather than a serial, and not classified by the programmers as drama), which share many of these conventions.

Finally, the programme has conventions of its own devising. These are acknowledged openly by a producer employed fourteen years after the inception of *Coronation Street* who boasts (or complains): 'You can't aim for realism . . . It's got a reality of its own . . . It's organic. It can survive anything. It generates itself' (in Thornber, 1974). This is not, of course, to suggest that these conventions are independent of either social belief or fictional custom, indeed they are usually best viewed in terms of an increased emphasis upon existing social and fictional convention. A modern writer on Victorian literary conventions suggests: 'For us, circumstantial authenticity is a conclusive test of realism, but for Victorian writers, fidelity to moral ideas was also important' (Reed, 1975, p. 4). *Coronation Street* would appear in this light to be Victorian since its most notable self-perpetuating convention is a reiterated demonstration of a belief in the fundamental warm-heartedness and solidarity of the industrial northern working classes. But the programme is not, of course, Victorian. The truth is that all forms of Realism demand this 'fidelity to moral ideas'.

Of course, this belief in the essential good-heartedness of 'ordinary people' occurs in other contemporary fictions, but it is so marked in *Coronation Street* that it becomes a convention in its own right. That the convention is a paradigmatic illustration of Joan Rockwell's contention (Rockwell, 1974, chapter 3) that the fidelity of Realism is a fidelity to the norms of a society rather than to its actuality can be seen by comparing its expression in *Coronation Street* with the already wistfully nostalgic view of the industrial working classes of his childhood given by Richard Hoggart in his extremely influential book *The Uses of Literacy*, which was first published three years before *Coronation Street* started (Hoggart, 1957). This book captured a view of northern working-class life (as group-centred, warm-hearted, matriarchal, faintly comical) and by its success made more socially (even academically) respectable the already widespread myth that somewhere out there, remote from the metropolis and yet thereby nearer to the heart of England, is a society where blunt common sense and unsentimental affection raises people above the concerns of industrialisation, or unions, or politics, or consumerism.

This last claim already suggests another aspect of convention: conventions of omission are at least as important as conventions of inclusion, though they are, of course, more difficult to classify. In narrative terms the Soap-Opera Realism of programmes like *Coronation Street* conventionally excludes everything which cannot be seen to be caused by people who are plausibly allowed to be physically present within the positive conventions already mentioned. This means, in effect, that most social explanations, and all openly political ones, are omitted. The differing situations, the troubles or successes, of the various characters are explained largely in terms of their (innate) psychological make-up, occasionally attributed to luck.

29

Any selection of episodes of *Coronation Street* will confirm the existence of an amalgam of these 'hidden' conventions of Realism. The title itself sets the programme firmly in a North-country industrial town with its suggestion of nineteenth-century terrace houses; and the promise of the small-group world it contains (and the large-scale world of industry and politics it omits) is confirmed by the opening sequences shot over the roofs and the glimpse of The Rovers Return ('My place of worship', it was called in the first episode by Ena Sharples, a more consistently acid character then than now). The style of these shots, invariably moving from this long-shot with its suggestion that this is a God's-eye view of the totality of experience, to a mid-shot ground-level view of the street, with its suggestion of the group, to a closer (but not usually close-up) view of some door or interior in Coronation Street, insists on typicality, insists that Coronation Street is a randomly chosen street, one among many; that each house is a randomly chosen house, one among many; and that it can only be in the close examination of textural detail that differences are to be found.

From the first episode we are placed in the settings that the generic conventions of Soap-Opera Realism demand: the 'meeting places' of pub and shop are alternated with the kitchen/living-rooms of the Tanners and the Barlows, just as in the most recent episodes we may move from the Kabin to The Rovers Return to Brian and Gail's kitchen. The strength of the convention may be judged from the way in which Mike Baldwin's 'factory' is 'domesticated' to a home where three women gossip over their sewing machines. Indeed, when the programme wants to show distress it is enough to move a character from these settings: the normally comic Stan became pathetic when stranded by the dual carriage-way; Deirdre's suicide plans were emphasised by placing her behind the girders of a bridge over the motorway or by a canal. Even the locking of a door, as when Bet shut herself off from her neighbours at the death of her unknown son, is a signal that the normally 'public' nature of rooms is changed, and that the environment (here to be glossed as life) is no longer to be trusted. Indeed we are rarely shown rooms that are not publicly available. Characters tend to be shown in bed only when they are in hospital, and bedrooms themselves are shown only when they become areas of access, as when Len needs to go through Elsie's room to get into the roof-space.

In the same way the appurtenances of the environment play a part in the 'generic hoax' of Realism. Tony Warren describes how his designer works to find a suitable bench for the pub (Warren, op. cit., p. 62) and obvious care is taken to distinguish one home from another. The private quarters at the pub, or any of the homes, all maintain the central image of the table, and deploy around it the variations of décor and appurtenances which, in the Realist genre proper, constitute fundamental indications of character. So we are told of Mrs Walker's pretentiousness by the ostentatious good taste of her china, of Ken's early class aspirations by his fastidious rejection of his father's offer of the sauce-bottle, of Hilda Ogden's vulgarity by her mural (and its mispronunciation) and her skein of pottery geese, of Ernie Bishop's suspect masculinity by his buttoned cardigan.

It is interesting to see the way in which a genre so firmly based upon the celebration of the regional deploys *linguistic* indicators to display a range of *moral* positions. All the characters (with the exception of comers-in like Mike Baldwin) use, of course, some variant of the local accent, but the variations, both between and within characters, are vital. Ken Barlow's Received Standard is used to establish him as an impartial arbiter of moral rectitude, whereas his uncle Albert Tatlock's broader Lancashire may sometimes be granted folk-wisdom but never an unbiased objectivity. Annie Walker, whose accent was much broader in the early days of the programme, has become more domineering as her accent has become refined, and it is this change of accent which is the chief indication that she is not now merely one of the crowd. Yet when she is to be shown as less reliable than her more homely colleagues she will be given some parodically posh phrase (' "Ebullient" we would say') that 'reveals' her falsity. Equally Hilda, another fluctuating character, is usually shown to be feckless partly by the broadness of her accent (broadness being less socially acceptable for women than for men); but when sympathy, even dignity, is to be given to her, this is often signalled by granting her an astute (if comic) readiness with words. So, questioned mockingly about her use of a phrase like 'It's us environment', she wins *morally* as well as linguistically by an explanation superb in its varying metaphorical as in its literal aptness: 'Us environment? It's what we live in, like goldfish in a goldfish bowl.' Or, belittled after an insult with the smooth admonition that she takes things too personally, she asserts a momentary superiority with the tart rejoinder: 'That's what insults is – personal.'

In terms of character the programme shows clearly its origins in Social Realism. Here fiction (like Hoggart's documentary) is true to the norms of the working class rather than the realities. 'The important thing about the working class,' as H.G. Wells put it, 'is to get out of it.' In Social Realism almost everyone does just that. The programme has deployed a whole series of petty bourgeois characters – Ray Langton, the Faircloughs, Renee Roberts, Ernest, even Stan (and Eddie Yeats?) are self-employed; Alf Roberts, Elsie Howard and Steve lower managerial; Ken Barlow on the fringe of the professional classes. The women cluster round the 'clean' service industries – Mavis, Betty, Bet, Suzie, Gail. Only Hilda Ogden of the long-standing characters is of the working class proper, joined recently by two women factory workers and one night-shiftman – and in his case the genre demands that we do not see him at work. Yet by its insistence the programme manages so well to *seem* to be about the working class that even such obviously bourgeois characters as Mike Baldwin are seen as deviant members of the working class, rather than as members of another fraction.

The generic demands of soap opera with regard to character are equally well observed. The peremptory requirement that there should be substantial roles for women is certainly fulfilled. Asked to name the important characters in *Coronation Street* most people would certainly put Ena Sharples, Annie Walker, Elsie Tanner (Howard), Hilda Ogden near the top of the list. And one would need to add Rita and Mavis, Betty and Bet before one came to consider any men. The sexual disposition of characters raises a problem for such a programme since two demands of the genre are to some extent incompatible: stereotyping would seem to demand that women should be weak and dependent on their men-folk; while the requirement of centrality for women means that they must be assertive at least in their 'visibility', if not in their roles. The programme resolves this problem artfully. Primarily its method is to deploy female characters in roles which themselves stereotypically stand outside the most common stereotype of the dependent, kindly female. In the most general sense the alliance of soap opera with Social Realism, with its stress on the working class, helps here, since working-class women have stereotypically been allowed to be much stronger characters than their middle-class equivalents. In the more particular sense there are specific sub-groups where the female stereotypes are figures of independence. These include older generation, preferably pre-1914, characters whose independence is seen as a survival from another age (Ena Sharples, say); the pub landlady whose occupation demands a 'masculine' hardheadedness (Annie Walker); women no-better-than-they-should-be, whose grasping of sexual experience is seen – still stereotypically – as a contradiction of the prevailing feminine stereotype (the earlier Elsie Tanner, Rita or, more recently, Suzie); the barmaids, whose very occupation is held to make them traditionally a hard-hitting, at once cynical yet vulnerable sub-set of the preceding group (Bet, and indeed Betty, both of whom have concealed illegitimate children); the widow or spinster of whom 'life' stereotypically demands a 'masculine' reaction (one is tempted to cite every woman in the programme, but Mavis, as the timid spinster, is the most testing example – saved by her own, again stereotypical, halting tenacity from being swamped by the world).

Much of the skill of the programme (and of the success of the genre) can be seen in the way in which it omits what is sociologically the normative grouping of mother, father, two children, while still managing to assert that it is about just such groups. It is difficult to think of children with two parents on the spot recently: Ken's son has been living with his grandmother in Scotland, Deirdre brings up her daughter alone, Gail has been brought up by her mother alone, Suzie left home because her parents were intolerable – only Brian lived with two parents (until he too left after a quarrel – though now, of course, he is married). In earlier days Elsie Tanner brought up her children alone, her pregnant daughter's first appearance presented her as someone about to leave her husband, Betty's illegitimate son was brought up by her sister, Bet never saw her son. But one is never conscious of this when watching the programme, because it insists repeatedly (impudently) that it is about the *family*, and the word itself, and the kitchen table which repeatedly symbolises it, have such powerful connotations that we are left, as viewers, unable to question it.

In terms of narrative management the programme fits the genre pattern of Soap-Opera Realism perfectly. As Christine Geraghty points out, each episode weaves together two or three events (Ken's girlfriend/Elsie Tanner's missing two-shilling piece/mislaid Christmas cards, say; or Fred Gee's fine/the Ken-Deirdre-Billy Walker triangle) and the apparent randomness, the suspended completions, the constant moves (often as many as ten changes of focus in one episode) suggest that the survey of life is a complete one. One feature peculiar to the serial-without-end is, of course, that it can convey better than any other form the sense that no 'conclusion' is final. It was always a part of nineteenth-century Classical Realism that character should appear to escape complete knowledge and predictability, and by this very elusiveness claim to be closer to reality. The serial form allows this elusiveness to go beyond character into the seemingly more solid 'reality' of event.

More negatively, the genre combination does not permit 'explanations' or resolutions of events in any terms other than personal ones. The strike of painters and decorators was not caused by any generalised distress at exploitation but by individual chagrin when two men were caught out using the firm's time and materials for work on the side. Stan was returned home to Hilda not because his economic situation does not allow anything else but because his brother-in-law tired of his sponging.

Indeed, it is an interesting feature of the programme that these Soap-Opera Realist conventions of narrative omission become clear to the viewer only when the programme makes some attempt to remedy the omissions. When (as in late 1974-5) the programme takes up an issue like unemployment, one becomes uncomfortably aware that the attempt to treat this in the personal terms which are all that the genre allows (Len's lack of orders/Fred looking for a job, Betty and Bet giving in their notices) is inadequate. If Northern Ireland is *not* mentioned the programme successfully hides the gap: if it *is* mentioned as the incidental way in which Bet's son was killed then one is conscious of the trivialisation which presents that death as the result of a car accident, an absolutely literal instance of the attribution of social events to the operation of chance.

Usually, however, the programme succeeds in persuading one of its completeness despite its reduction of most situations to being about getting a partner in life. And the phrase 'in life' does convey the appropriate feeling, even though the programme contains a few life-long liaisons. Only dead husbands or wives do not disappear – or die. Jack Walker's photo remains on the mantelpiece, but other partners pop in and out with astonishingly fertile excuse. The most casual viewer would know of Deirdre's being engaged to Billy Walker, married to Ray Langton, courted by Ken Barlow, back on the market; and yet while these episodes go on they are 'happy ever after' situations, partly because that is the vocabulary and style which is used for their presentation, and partly because a serial, and especially a serial as uniquely long-running as this, can both allow time to forget and rely on a fluctuating audience. Len Fairclough has been a suitor for almost every woman in the programme. Rita alternates as Len's wife and someone he needs to court because she is being wooed by someone else. The process can be seen at its limit with the case of Elsie Tanner who, about to become a grandmother as the first programme opened, is still, eighteen years later, the object of a procession of suitors, variously glamorous or homely, each one of whom is presented as a possible 'permanent' partner. One awaited with a tingle of anticipation the moment when that most permanent of wives, Emily, her mourning over, was either returned to the marriage market or given up to insulated old age. (Now, of course, she has remarried, to a bigamist.) These are the only stereotypes of role available.

The force of this expectation of domesticity and of romantic love mundanely distilled through a sieve of everyday life can be seen when the programme attempts to depart from the convention. Such episodes as Ernie's murder, or the accident with the lorry and its dramatic consequences, are never satisfactorily digested and usually end with the event tailing lamely away. Indeed their lack of 'fit' can be seen most clearly in the programme makers' own sense that they must change the stylistic conventions of the serial form (as delineated in Christine Geraghty's paper) to fit the insertion of an unexpected theme. The uncharacteristically melodramatic lorry accident failed to conform to the general formal expectations of either timing or picking up of suspense points, in that time did *not* elapse naturalistically between episodes, and the 'cliffhanger' *was* picked up at exactly the point at which it had been left. Ernie's funeral led similarly to a programme almost unique in its singleness of plot line. Such events never manage the 'naturalness' of Hilda's borrowing of a négligé for her second honeymoon, or of Mavis' repeatedly disappointed *amours*.

As for the programme's own convention, the view it takes of northern industrial working-class life, 'the fascinating freemasonry' as Tony Warren saw it, this is so forceful an imperative that it dominates all others. Indeed, the programme can best be thought of as a set of variations on this theme. The introduction of outsiders or the departure of insiders is invariably the signal for disruption, a disruption healed only by the closing of ranks. So Annie Walker's social aspirations, comically though they are presented, are warmly cherished, whereas her invasive cousin's aspirations are morally condemned when they emerge as borrowing from neighbours. Hilda Ogden, so often deplored, becomes an object of sympathetic help from every neighbour when her husband disappears. When Deirdre ventured as far from home as the local evening institute's Keep Fit classes she was sexually assaulted in the street. Billy Walker's returns from Jersey are always a signal for disturbance.

This last example illustrates, too, another aspect of this view of northern working-class life, whereby the neighbourhood grouping is seen to be more important than the family grouping. The family that the programme is essentially about is Coronation Street, not a nuclear family. Mrs Sharples condemned the whole world beyond as pretentious and unreliable when in the very first programme she dismissed the obviously physically near but emotionally foreign Esmerelda Street with the withering 'Very bay-window down there'. The anonymous children who occasionally play in the street behind the credit titles are more important than the 'real' children of Len, say, or Hilda or Elsie, who rarely appear. The matriarchies that the programme celebrates are the matriarchies of place, not of blood relationship: Annie Walker's pub is her family; Elsie mothered the 'daughters' she had taken in; and Ena Sharples and, earlier, Minnie Caldwell, are grandmothers to the street, with that combination of sentimentality and trustworthiness traditionally (stereotypically) accorded to such legendary figures.

Above all, the ethos is that of nostalgia for vanished virtues. The 'documentary' tone has always been so modulated as to suggest an attempt to capture for posterity a vanishing world. Tony Warren speaks in his memoir of Eric Spier's 'haunting signature tune' (op. cit., p. 57) and it is in nothing more haunting than in its resemblance to 'Thanks for the Memory'. Even the earliest programmes were full of proud boasts about not being up-to-date: one character explained, 'I've never learned the "phone" ', and Ena Sharples deplored the 'modern' tendency to cremation. She is still deploring change today, dismissing frozen foods as 'mostly muck', or modern morality as undisguised selfishness.

There has been over the years, however, a tendency to make the view of this relic more sentimental than it was. The early programmes' shots behind the credit titles showed Coronation Street under a forbiddingly dark sky. Now the sun shines on it, as a cat curls up in contented sleep (finds, in other words, the comfort of home), and a tree blossoms in the back alley (signifying to us all the fragile beauty to be found in the most unlikely spots). The sops to modernity – Mike Baldwin's thrusting cockney business man, or Steve's rising young executive – do not take over the street but are taken over by its neighbourliness, so that we have Mike secretly paying part of Bet's rent for her share of Renee's house and Steve finding a job for Suzie (who has always treated him with scorn) when she was down on her luck. Early programmes were much readier to use as part of their Realism the washing drying round the fire or the constant background noise of the wireless. Now the occasional shots of fish and chips in newspaper on the table at the Ogdens are used to show the Ogdens as outsiders who let the side down by such sleaziness.

The conventions of Realism, some variants of which this paper has so far discussed, have long been a source of suspicion among critics. Even in the nineteenth-century heyday of Classical Realism there was a sceptical view that the implicit claim of Realism to be synonomous with reality was, if taken seriously, not to be trusted. As early as 1887 Trollope was asserting: 'The realistic must not be true, but just so far removed from the truth as to suit the erroneous idea of truth which the reader may be supposed to entertain' (in Reed, op. cit., p. 4). This distrust has grown in recent years. It springs from a belief that an audience will be naive enough to confuse Realism and reality. But here, it seems, it is the critics (who invented the term Realism) who are more naive than any audience. Even Barthes in his attack on Realism recognises that the quirky particularisations (of place, character, setting, motive) which form so essential a part of Realism may even suggest *un*reality: 'It is the very preciseness of the reference to the world which makes the function unreal: one encounters here the paradox of the art of the novel: any fashion so detailed becomes unreal' (Barthes, 1975, p. 38). His claim, of course, is that an audience is seduced into accepting this unreality as reality: 'The more contingent the function the more "natural" it seems' (ibid.).

Yet the individual's sense of the conventions can be seen in a response to the atypical event of the murder of Ernie Bishop when a phone-caller protested: 'You just shouldn't have killed off Ernie Bishop at all. This is a family programme and there shouldn't be violence. That kind of business is for the cops and robbers', and thereby echoed the misgivings of a script-writer who had expressed his concern that it was 'a bit cops-and-robbers, a bit Sweeney-ish.'* More generally, and more positively, the popular audience's awareness in practice of many of these conventions (however reluctant they may be to express them as theory) can scarcely be denied in view of the success of such a parody of the genre as is presented weekly on the Saturday morning children's programme *Tiswas*. Here, under the title 'Crossdale Street', one sees displayed, to the obvious satisfaction of a non-academic audience, a parodic distillation of the conventions of Soap-Opera Realism. A typical (2-minute) episode, for example, shows an old-fashioned, middle-aged, working-class couple, the woman in curlers at her wooden-rollered mangle, the man in collarless shirt chewing stolidly over his newspaper at the kitchen table. The episode involves a row over trivial infidelities with the woman shouting abuse in accents variously Mummerset and North-country at the indifferent back of the man, who is finally forced to pay attention when she empties a mixing bowl over his head.

Here we see a programme using the conventions of Soap-Opera Realism: the settling-in-life theme for those clearly already settled; the conclusive but not final ending; the sexual, social and age stereotyping of the strident, excitable female and the phlegmatic and obtuse male; the ostensibly commonplace but flagrantly outdated setting. And the programme makers are able to do this in the confidence that their viewers will be so familiar with the conventions as conventions that they will see the fun of their being caricatured. And even more importantly one should note the comedy that the parody achieves by having the picture partially obscured for more than half

---

* Quoted by Stephen Hancock in *Death on the Street,* shown on ITV on 24 July 1979.

the episode by the rolling of a seemingly endless list of comic credits, because the comedy here is dependent on the pointing of a shared knowledge that the originals of the parody display their own unreality by running such credits very obtrusively across the ending of each episode. The conventions of Realism are by definition 'hidden' in one sense, but *Coronation Street* does not seek to hide them (or at least not all of them) in any absolute sense.

Part of *Coronation Street*'s success lies, I have suggested, in its ability to combine happily a straight use of Realism with an unpatronising if sly acknowledgment (via such devices as the self-conscious playing up of nostalgia or North-countryness) that the audience will recognise the tricks of the trade. Another part of its success lies in its happy mingling of the conventions of other genres whose methods depend on open display – the Ivor Novello strain in Warren's art.

First, from the beginning the programme has taken (and conveyed) a childlike pleasure in using the 'arty' linking devices of 40s films. For example, talk of a set of characters is immediately followed by shots of them in action. So, in the first episode the warning given to Florrie Lindley that she should not extend credit to the Tanners was followed by scenes of the Tanner family at home squabbling about money, or, recently, talk of Gail's broken engagement was followed by shots of her mooning about the café. Or the link of the reflection of the same scene with different characters is used, as when we move from Annie Walker's discussion of the merits of different forms of protein to Stan sitting over his meat and potato pie and baked beans. The device is used quite openly, often indeed comically, as though to correct any lurking confusion between Realism and reality, and to remind us of the artifice of art.

More importantly the programme continuously mingles a huge (and I would claim overt) use of caricature along with its depiction of Realist characters. Almost any character except the adolescent ones (who are in many ways out of place in a narrative so conscientiously old-fashioned as to predate the very concept of adolescence) may be subject to this, but the ones who most consistently appear in this way are Ena Sharples and, currently, Annie Walker. Mrs Sharples has always been treated in this way from the moment of her aggressive self-introduction: 'I'm a widow woman.' There is nothing of Realism in the hugely square face or the large mesh hairnet clamped in place with metal pins. She may have changed her nature from the acerbic comic eccentric to the infallible gnomic grandmother, but her style has always been that of the caricature. Annie Walker, in the early days a creature of Realism, has been increasingly written up into caricature, occasionally going right over the top with statements like "tis caviar to the general', and then taken down by a ripost of self-caricatured vulgarity, as when her claim (apropos of *crême bruté* and *petit pot au chocolat*), 'good taste is such a rare commodity', is followed by Bet's rejoinder: 'I never got beyond bacon butties and egg and chips.' Stereotyping contributes to this too, since the programme sometimes guys its own use of hidden 'stereotype', by having characters play the stereotype rather than be it. So Bet, in the normal run of the programme a stereotype of the tarty barmaid (with of course a stereotypical heart of gold), will often act a parody of the type – offering her bosom or her company in a caricature of the common or the promiscuous.

The third element from different and more open genres, of which the programme makes use, is in its deployment of comic dialogue. There is a Realist background dialogue of unremarkable commonplaceness, but frequently the conversation erupts either into a stylised repartee, distinguished only by the class accents from that of brittle West End social comedy, or the language of the stand-up comic. As examples of the first one may take Eddie Yeats' comment on Mrs Walker's claim to be fastidious that he is 'just as fast, not quite as 'ideous'; or Mrs Sharples' exchange: 'What religion are you then?' — 'I don't really know much about it.' — 'Oh I see . . . C of E.'

The comic patter is on the same lines but goes further with its suggestion of the straight man and the comic in encounters such as Ray's attempted pick-up: 'Why don't you sit down for a bit?' – 'A bit of what?'; or its use of deliberately vulgar double entendre in the manner of McGill postcards, as in Elsie's suggestive disclaimer: 'It might be some time since I last ran up a trouser leg.' Sometimes it takes on the virtuoso tone of a Beryl Reid solo as in Ena Sharples' monologue on funerals: 'Where're you being buried? Whatever you do don't go to that Crematorium down at the bottom. As the coffin rolls away they play "Moonlight and Roses". I spoke to the Superintendent personally. 'E said: "That's not "Moonlight and Roses", that's "Andantina"." I just took one look at him and said back: "Andantina" or no "Andantina", *I'm* rolling away to the tune of "Crimond".' Clearly this is totally redundant in Realist terms of naturalism, but perfectly acceptable in the world of *Coronation Street*.

These departures from Realist convention are not, of course, random ones. Any genre which encourages background stereotyping with the foregrounding of particularities already comes close to caricature. There was the same persistent tendency in the nineteenth-century Realism of Dickens to spill over into caricature. The more fashionable twentieth-century variants of Realism deny themselves caricature by their concentration on psychological depth. *Coronation Street*, in its self-consciously old-fashioned approach, usually eschews such inner searching.

The comic routines and the vulgar postcard jokes are at home, too, even in a Realist world, when the Realist world is that of the northern working class, which still sends such postcards home from the seaside, and in whose well patronised working-men's clubs the stand-up comic (as likely as not a woman), whose stock-in-trade is the conversational ad lib, often with a 'feed' sitting (in mock Realist fashion) in the audience, traditionally makes a living. Moreover, the image of character that the Realist world of *Coronation Street* wishes to present fits remarkably well with the world-view embodied in the northern club comic, who presents a character sharp yet not slick, always with an eye to the main chance but not uncharitable, wryly aware that one may well appear craggily foolish to the bland world outside and must, therefore, hit out first. This kind of supposedly defensive fossil group may, in a programme like *Coronation Street*, twice weekly, celebrate its own virtues, and forestall attack by appearing to be its own most astute critic.

These departures from strict Realism are made acceptable by being departures on the one hand into a closely allied genre, and on the other into a genre which, though differing dramatically in *method* from Social Realism, largely shares its *viewpoint*. None the less they *are* departures, and clearly make suspect any case that *Coronation Street* pretends to be synonomous with life.

My argument then is that *Coronation Street*, though deploying the devices of the Soap-Opera Realism upon which it is based, far from attempting to hide the artifice of these devices (other than by the generic imperative to hide) rather asks us to take pleasure in its artistry, much as a stage magician will not show us how his tricks are done yet never claims (other than by the generic imperative to claim) that he has *actually* sawn a woman in half.

TERRY LOVELL

Ideology and *Coronation Street*

1. WHY IDEOLOGY?

It is commonplace among Marxists and non-Marxists alike to make a divide between 'high' and 'popular' culture, and to discuss the latter in terms of its social determinants and functions. This can be seen as much in the work of Q.D. Leavis on popular fiction (Leavis, 1965) as it can in Frankfurt Marxism, for instance. The category which is most often used by Marxists for this purpose of identifying the social bearings of popular entertainment is that of ideology. While there have been fairly radical developments in the theory of ideology which have to some extent redefined that term, the assumption that the work of producing popular entertainment is also and at the same time the production of ideology has continued virtually unchallenged through all these changes in the theory of ideology. It is an assumption which unites otherwise diametrically opposed schools of Marxist cultural studies.

In this essay I want to question that assumption, and to examine the limits within which the concept of ideology may usefully be applied in the analysis of a popular television series such as *Coronation Street*. I shall be concerned with two kinds of limitation. Firstly, popular forms have class-related dimensions which cannot be captured and analysed within a catch-all concept of ideology without stretching that concept to the point of uselessness. And secondly, the concept of ideology was developed in connection with the class co-ordinates of thought and culture. Sex and gender are equally important points of reference for the analysis of popular culture, yet it is questionable whether the concept of ideology can be simply extended to include sex-related cultural domination in addition to that of class, without considerable modification of the theory which informs that concept.

The concept of ideology has become debased coinage – part of the small change of contemporary intellectual currency. Yet in its origins it was less ubiquitous, and to that extent more valuable.* It was developed to indicate that ideas were not free-floating products of the mind, but were rooted in politics and society. Within Marxist theory this was sharpened into the claim that the ideas which people hold are a function of class position and class

---

* For an account of the origins and development of the concept, see S. Hall, 'The Hinterland of Science. Ideology and the "Sociology of Knowledge" ', *Cultural Studies*, No. 10, 1977.

interest. The theory of ideology sketchily present in the work of Marx and Engels is part of a broader attempt to discover and specify the social determinants of ideas, and to relate the adequacy or inadequacy of those ideas to those social determinants and functions.

2. THEORIES OF IDEOLOGY: A CONTINUUM

There are two positions associated with the concept of ideology, each of which finds some legitimation in the writings of Marx and Engels. Firstly, the concept of ideologies as discrete and opposed world-views which are rooted in the differential placing of social classes within the structure of social relations, and the different experiences, activities and interests which result. Secondly, the concept of ideological domination – the use of ideas by the dominant class to further their domination. These concepts are not necessarily opposed. Rather they are extreme positions on a continuum. Different theories of ideology may be located on this continuum by their relative distance from each pole.

At one extreme, approached by Georg Lukács, dominant and oppositional ideologies are posited (Lukács, 1968). Lukács, as is well known, identified the proletariat as *the* epistemologically privileged class. It occupied that position in the social structure from which it was both possible and necessary to develop an adequate view of the whole. The class interests of the proletariat, unlike those of the bourgeoisie, required that their thought and consciousness penetrate beyond the fetishised forms of capitalist social relations, to the essential reality – that which they are forms *of*. Lukács gave no account of the mechanisms of ideological production – neither its institutions and processes, nor the intellectual work it entailed. The move from class position to class consciousness was not made problematic. Economic crisis was its automatic motor. Given class position and interest, the production of a totalising ideology followed more or less spontaneously when the time was ripe. What interested Lukács was whether or not a class was capable of generating a 'totalising ideology' – an ability which depended on its characteristics *as* a class and on the political imperatives dictated by its class interests, rather than upon more mundane questions of its access to, control over, and competence to use, the means of ideological production. The question of the ability of one class to impose its 'world-view' upon another through its monopoly of such access and control also scarcely arose for Lukács.

Different world-views were discrete and insulated for Lukács, to be related only to their social base in class interest, rather than to each other, or to the conditions of their own production. Yet Marx and Engels had written that: 'The ideas of the ruling class are, in every age, the ruling ideas' (Marx and Engels, 1970, p. 61). The dominant class which controls the means of production will also control the means of ideological production. It will deploy those means and resources to ensure the dissemination of ideas

41

which serve its own class interests, and the suppression of oppositional world-views, so that the thought of the dominated will become structured not by, or not only by, its own class interests, but also by the categories of the dominant ideology which naturalise the existing, fetishised forms of capitalism as eternal and necessary.

Lukács mainly wrote about bourgeois thought, and identified its limits in the limits of bourgeois class interest. For him, oppositional ideologies are (relatively) unproblematic. Lukács does create space in his theory where they might be made problematic. For class position and class interest determine for Lukács not the actual historical consciousness of a given social class, but its 'imputed' consciousness. This is an ideal type. It is that consciousness which a class would have were it fully cognisant of its own class interests, of everything which impinged upon those interests, and fully rational in pursuit of them. This gives the space which Lukács requires for a certain distance between the ideal, imputed consciousness of a class, and its actual consciousness at any moment. Imputed consciousness is determined entirely by class position and class interest. But the actual historical consciousness which a class has achieved at any point in time may fall well short of this ideal imputed consciousness, and historical consciousness *is* open to other determinations of the kind omitted from Lukács' theory, including the constraints of ideological domination. But while Lukács left this space, he made no attempt to fill it. Clearly he believed that in the long run, when the contradictions of the social relations of production reached crisis proportions, and the time was ripe for revolution, the distance between actual and imputed consciousness would be bridged, and the two would converge.

Lukács' intellectual energies were entirely directed towards theorising the determinants of imputed rather than historical consciousness. Given the course of twentieth-century history, and the obstinate persistence and even widening of the gap between imputed and historical consciousness, subsequent Marxist theorists have been compelled to pay more attention to the determinants of historical consciousness and, in so doing, to question the validity of this kind of division between ideal and actual.

The other pole of the continuum is most nearly approached at the present time by Althusser's theory of 'ideology in general' (Althusser, 1977). He transforms ideology, with the aid of Lacan's theory of psychoanalysis, into a theory of the production of the experiencing, acting human subject. As a result, all subjectivity, experience and action are, so to speak, caught within the space of 'ideology in general' and radically separated off from the processes of *knowledge* production. (For Lukács there could be no absolutely hard and fast distinction between knowledge and ideology, since both were a function of class consciousness.) Ideology (in general) is shifted perceptibly away from the realm of ideas by Althusser. It becomes the production, through representation, of a particular *effect* – that of recognition. The individual human subject is constituted in and through ideology, and (mis)recognises itself, and its imagined relationship to real social relations.

42

S/he (mis)recognises who s/he is, what the world is, and his/her place within it.

Ideology in general is an abstraction which exists concretely only in and through particular ideologies for Althusser, and particular ideologies *are* subject to the processes of ideological domination. Therefore it is the categories of the dominant ideology which so deeply inform the consciousness/unconsciousness and self-identity of the individual human subjects constituted by ideology-in-general. Althusser, in his later writings (Althusser, 1976, 1977), makes frequent references to oppositional ideologies. Yet his appropriation of 'the lived' – of consciousness, action and experience – for ideology in general leaves him very little room to account for the existence of these oppositional ideologies in any but *ad hoc* fashion. Thus in the case of Lukács at one pole, the problem is to theorise ideological domination, while at the other, Althusser is faced by the danger of making that domination total and inescapable, because built into our very language, perception and self-identity.

The link between the two is to be found in the work of Gramsci (1971). Gramsci drew the theory of ideology away from its exclusive concern with ideas, by drawing attention to the practices within which they were embedded, and the effects which they have. He was particularly interested in those ideas which had their roots in day-to-day practical activities, and which found expression in common-sense thinking rather than in more systematic bodies of thought. He also drew attention to the structured social institutions which functioned to support the hegemony of the dominant class. It is this emphasis on ideas as they are 'lived' which Althusser has taken from Gramsci. However, while Gramsci argues that the most powerful ideologies are those which are 'lived' in action, Althusser reverses that proposition, so that whatever is 'lived' is by that token ideological. He thus closes off for himself an avenue which Gramsci left open; he cannot posit any relationship between 'the lived' and *knowledge* – especially that knowledge of the social formation which must inform successful revolutionary challenges.

Gramsci allows for a considerable *lack* of fit between experience, consciousness, and the categories of domination, which could feed into knowledge production. For Gramsci, common-sense thinking was a mishmash of received notions, truisms, reflections on experience, etc. It is always contradictory, and always deeply contaminated by the categories of the dominant ideology. But he recognised a substratum of 'good sense' within this contradictory amalgam of common sense. Common sense is the repository of the hopes, fears and aspirations of the dominant, as well as of the naturalised status quo of domination. It is because it is not any one consistent thing that common sense cannot be fully appropriated for the dominant ideology, any more than its basis, the practical activity and experience of the dominated, can be. Gramsci recognised very clearly that even 'good sense' is inadequate to the needs of a revolutionary movement and to the requirements of knowledge production and of revolutionary action.

Gramsci differed from Lukács in the interest which he had in the institutional structure of ideological production, but shares with him a strong sense of its differential class base. He shares with Althusser on the other hand a concern with domination and control through ideological production, but differs from him in refusing to allow 'the lived' and the terms of common-sense thinking to be wholly appropriated for dominance, to lose their close links with unrecuperable elements in the experience of the dominated.

The move along the continuum from Lukács through Gramsci to Althusser involved a broadening of the concept of ideology. Lukács is traditionalist in maintaining the identification of ideology with ideas. Gramsci differentiates ideas into those which are developed as abstract general systems, and those which remain socially embedded and are expressed in action and in common sense. Althusser retains the former in his concept of 'theoretical ideologies', and extends the latter to include the production of 'the ideological effect', that of (mis)recognition. I have discussed Althusser's concept of ideology at length elsewhere (Lovell, 1980), and will not pursue it further here. But it must be questionable whether the same concept can be stretched to cover so much – the manner in which people 'live' their relationship to social relations, *and* the process of constituting individual human beings as subjects *and* complex bodies of abstract thought, *and* the truisms of common sense.

3. STRUCTURES OF FEELING AND SENSIBILITY

When the concept of ideology is extended to art and the mass media, then these problems are compounded. One of two things happens. Either the association of 'ideology' with ideas is retained, and art is reduced to its cognitive dimension (as is the case in Lukács' aesthetic writings) or the extra-cognitive dimensions of art are recognised, and the concept of ideology is extended to include them, and stretched as a result to the point of uselessness. Yet the problem which leads to this outcome is a real one which is not easily solved. The aesthetic and emotional effects of art and the media are as much, if not more, amenable to mobilisation in relation to class interest than are ideas. If the concept of ideology has been illegitimately extended here it is for the good reason that we lack the terms necessary for mapping out the effects of art on to class and politics, and ideology is the best we have. Equally clearly a single concept cannot stand in for so much. I believe that the concept of ideology is best restricted to something close to its original referent – that is to say, to ideas which are inadequate in ways which can be related to the motivations of the class struggle – wherever those ideas are located (abstract theory, common sense, art, the mass media).

It follows that we need to develop a further vocabulary for talking about those class-related dimensions of art which cannot be reduced to ideas.

44

Raymond Williams' 'structure of feeling' is one possible candidate. For example, in discussing *Mary Barton*, Williams identifies two contrary 'structures of feeling' which were prevalent at the time and which inform Gaskell's novel. The first was a sympathetic identification with the appalling conditions and sufferings of the working class; the second, fear of working-class violence. He discusses the flaws and dislocations of the novel in terms of the contradictory play of these two structures (Williams, 1958). This concept is useful in so far as it avoids the reduction of literature to its ideas, which is the usual consequence of the use of the concept of ideology to discuss the class bearings of literature. But Williams has been criticised for a certain blindness to literary form. For instance, in his interesting *Country and the City* (Williams, 1973), he moves from the analysis of poetry to novels, without registering the difference in his analysis. Even when he limits himself to a single form, his analysis runs up against similar problems. The literary form which is the bearer of his 'structures of feeling' is itself a structure and not of feeling. How do the formal and aesthetic properties of the work limit its structures of feeling? What other constraints, over and above the constraints of structure of feeling itself, determine and limit the properties of those formal structures? For instance, the available means and conditions of cultural production itself, the historically developed conventions available, etc. How do these various sets of constraints combine with more strictly ideological determinations?

Williams' concept might perhaps be complemented by a notion of 'structures of sensibility' which could also be identified and described in class terms, and which would allow us to raise questions about the historically established class properties of aesthetic form, and how those class properties are established and maintained. In the case of high bourgeois art, factors such as monopolies on education and cultural history are of obvious importance. In other cases, the appropriateness of certain forms to certain class values and habits may be involved. Richard Hoggart raises some of these questions in relation to working-class forms of art and entertainment (Hoggart, 1957). But in general the work of locating cultural forms in class terms has scarcely begun.

The project of developing an ideological analysis of a popular television series such as *Coronation Street* depends on the prior identification of the available ideological space within which it operates. It has been argued that it is an error to try to identify the ideology of a work outside of its production within the work in question, as something independent of work which the work 'expresses', or 'reflects'. But the restriction of 'ideology' in a work to the ideas which it carries, combined with the recognition that it is not the ideas of a work which define its existence as a cultural artefact, circumvents this objection, while at the same time limiting the scope and importance of purely ideological analysis of such works. For the identity and relationship between ideas in television series, films, political tracts, common sayings, etc. can be acknowledged and explored without losing sight of the specificity of

45

each. They may be bearers and creators of a common or overlapping ideology, without thereby becoming indistinguishable from one another, because their specificity is not contained in their ideas – although the manner in which those ideas are produced within and through particular 'signifying practices' may well be specific to each. The remaining point in the objection, that these various cultural forms do not merely reflect already existing ideologies but themselves construct ideology, may be readily conceded. Ideas may well be developed for the first time in a novel rather than in a sociology journal. By and large, however, this is not the case, and the ideas which can be extracted from even the most progressive and complex work are often rather commonplace. An awareness of the commonplaces of ideological thought outside the works of popular entertainment under analysis will certainly be necessary for the identification of the ideological dimensions of that work.

4. IDEOLOGY, SEX AND GENDER

There is a further problem in using the concept of ideology in the analysis of popular entertainment. 'Ideology' is a concept which is based on categories of class and class domination and oppression. But all popular entertainment, and especially soap opera, draws upon and produces ideas, structures of feeling and sensibility which cluster around sex and gender differences, domination and oppression, as well as class. Again the difficulty arises from the attempt to extend the concept outside its original connotations in an *ad hoc* way. For while it has become common to speak of 'patriarchal ideology', this usage cuts across classifications of ideology along class lines, and the exact relationship between class and sex, ideology and patriarchy has yet to be determined. The Women's Liberation Movement has led to the exploration of the relationship between class and sex in capitalist society, and there is an impressive and growing literature which is beginning to open up this and related questions. But this is work in progress, and few people would claim that the relationship between the two is now fully understood. Any discussion of the sex and gender co-ordinates of a popular serial like *Coronation Street* will implicitly assume some analysis or another of the relationship between class and sex under capitalism, and making that analysis explicit would involve going far beyond the scope of the present essay. But at least it should be possible to give some indication of the kinds of issue which need to be taken into consideration in such an analysis.

(i) The Context of Cultural Production

It is commonly assumed that because cultural production is capitalist commodity production, the ideological credentials of these products are automatically secured for dominance and the reproduction of existing social relations. This assumption informed the cultural pessimism of the Frankfurt School, and is still very widespread (Murdock and Golding, 1973). I have argued (op. cit.) that no such implication can be drawn from the penetration of capital into cultural production, and the consequent transformation of its product into commodities.

In the first chapter of *Capital*, Marx analyses the twofold nature of the commodity, as *use-value* (the repository of useful attributes which the purchaser of the commodity gains access to and uses), and *value* (the repository of definite amounts of human labour expended in their production). With the exception of the commodity labour-power, Marx does not analyse the use-value of any of the commodities produced under capitalism. It would be impossible to specify the use-values of a commodity like a television series without considerable theoretical and empirical investigation of a kind for which Marx provides no guidance. Yet it is only when consumed as use-values by individuals that any ideological function is performed by such commodities for capitalism. We have absolutely no theoretical grounds for supposing that the use-values consumed are identical, or even commensurate with, the ideological requirements of capitalism.

We can assume that while people watch entertainment programmes like *Coronation Street* in order to be entertained rather than in order to meet the ideological needs of capitalism, yet entertainment is unlikely to be ideologically neutral for all that. Entertainment is not primarily a vehicle for the transmission of ideas. But even the most emotionally saturated entertainment will also produce ideas, and these will certainly be locatable in terms of ideology. What determines the ideological parameters of popular entertainment? Various essays in this collection look at some of these determinants. For example, Paterson examines the production context of *Coronation Street* for the constraints which this context places upon the programme makers, while Jordan looks at the conventions of realism and of soap opera for their ideological consequences, and these are both important areas of ideological determination. What I would like to add here is a consideration of the ways in which the constraints upon producers to create use-values associated with entertainment limits their ability to produce at the same time a commodity which meets the ideological requirements of capitalism. This particular set of constraints operates in the opposite direction to those identified by Paterson and Jordan, and it would not be possible in abstraction to know what the outcome of these contradictory pulls would be in any given case, without close analysis of the actual programmes produced. But clearly what I am saying supports the contention which underlies all the contributions to this work, that ideological production always occurs under contradictory pressures, and that its results are therefore never, or rarely, ideologically consistent and uni-dimensional.

We cannot assume, then, that the negotiation of the relationship between cultural production and ideological function *will* always be achieved. And even where it is, I would want to argue that the ideology of a work does not exhaust the class and sexual politics of that work, because the level of ideas is at best secondary in popular entertainment. The emotional and aesthetic

47

impact of a work of popular entertainment like *Coronation Street* would also have to be analysed. What I termed 'structures of feeling and sensibility' would have to be identified, and it might well be the case that these affect the viewer in ways which pull against its ideological resolutions.

Finally, whether we are concerned with ideology, or with structures of feeling and sensibility, it is necessary to avoid the temptation of mistaking what is *actually* achieved by particular production teams, and the limits within which they work in these respects, with what it is *possible* to do within any particular type of programme. Because the dominant structures of feeling and sensibility are reproduced in the programme, it does not follow that different structures of feeling and sensibility might not have been made much more prominent, *despite* the various constraints under which the programme makers worked. A good practical exercise for study groups would be to attempt to rewrite an episode or storyline for *Coronation Street* within the constraints of the genre, from a feminist or socialist perspective, without losing the qualities which make *Coronation Street* so pleasurable and popular. This would facilitate the discovery of the extent to which it is the constraints of genre, production context, etc. which determine the class and sex co-ordinates of the programme, and how far the entertainment values themselves are bound up with dominant ideologies/sensibilities. What kinds of change would be required to create greater space for the production of feminist and socialist sensibilities and ideas?

(ii) The Pleasure of the Text

Such an exercise would also depend upon a second important area of investigation – the sources of pleasure which *Coronation Street* draws upon, as its consistently high ratings testify. Geraghty's paper comes very evidently, as all useful work in this area must, from a long-standing and positive involvement with those pleasures. She identifies the typical narrative, plot and character structures within which *Coronation Street* in particular, and the long-running serial in general, operates. In so doing she identifies things which in themselves are a source of pleasure regardless of the ideological effects in whose service they may be mobilised.

Questions of the pleasure of the text relate most clearly to one aspect of the commodity, its use-value, while questions of ideology relate to the commodity's social functions. The interface between these two is, I would argue, always and necessarily an irregular one. Ideological analysis can identify the manner and extent to which those pleasures are mobilised for ideological functions. Use-value analysis will be able to identify the resistance which these commodities offer to that ideological role. This brings us back to the discussion of Gramsci in the first half of this essay. For I argued that the hopes, fears and aspirations of those who are oppressed within the structures of class and sex domination of contemporary society will find partial, confused and contradictory expression in such forms as common sense. It is precisely these things which will provide at least one important source of pleasure that producers of programmes of popular entertainment must meet if their commodities are to supply the use-values which lead people to purchase and consume them. We are therefore likely to find subversive, or at least unassimilable, elements within popular entertainment – what Dyer has called 'utopias' (Dyer, 1978) – as well as evidence of the categories of the dominant ideology, the naturalisation of the status quo.

What is at stake here goes beyond the strict reference of this paper (the ideology of popular culture) to the broader question of the *politics* of a pleasurable text. How is the process of signification, and the ideas and pleasures it produces, related to the class struggle? My argument is that the answer must be: in complex and contradictory ways. These cannot be contained within the category of ideology, whether this is specified in terms of *Cahiers du Cinéma*'s 'category A' films (those which allow clear passage to the dominant ideology), nor their remaining categories (those which in various ways block or deflect that passage) (Comolli and Narboni, 1971), nor in terms of the seepage through 'cracks and fissures', of intransigent oppositional ideologies.

The class and sex co-ordinates of a popular work are not unlike those of Gramsci's 'common sense'. Certainly one highly salient set of co-ordinates will be provided by the categories of the dominant ideology. Here the fact that popular entertainment is produced by people who are not, or are no longer, working-class must be relevant, as well as the nature of the conventional and production constraints under which they produce. All other things being equal, it is hardly surprising if producers operating within those constraints do so within additional limits created by their own class sensibility. Yet to all these constraints must be added those which producers are under to create programmes which are popular, as measured by audience ratings, and therefore to provide the use-values which that audience seeks in such entertainment. Some of the pleasures of entertainment will be readily mobilised for domination. Others may be more intractable. Among the latter will be those expressing the hopes and aspirations of the dominated which are thwarted under capitalism and patriarchy. To be sure, these will be deeply embedded alongside the contradictory sensibilities of domination, rather in the manner in which 'good sense' exists within 'common sense'. But their expression and development in however contradictory a manner within popular culture ensures that they remain alive and available for different mobilisations and articulations.

It would be foolish to find too much encouragement for revolutionary optimism in these ambivalent elements within popular entertainment. But it would be equally foolish to regard these too pessimistically, in isolation from other contexts. Revolutionary strategies obviously cannot be based on popular entertainment alone. But it is necessary to insist that because popular culture does not belong to the masses, feminism and revolution, it is not captured for reaction, patriarchy and domination either. Rather it is situated ambivalently and in contradictory ways, in relation to both. I should like to finish by attempting to map some of the ideas, pleasures and sensibilities of *Coronation Street* on to the politics of sex, rather than class.

5. CORONATION STREET, SOAP OPERA, AND THE POLITICS OF SEX

Here I am mainly concerned with what I have termed the 'structures of feeling and sensibility' of *Coronation Street* as they relate to sexual politics.

Jordan's essay raises the question of how the demands of the conventions of soap opera for strong, dominant women characters is squared with the demands of patriarchal ideology. She examines the manner in which this contradiction is negotiated in the typical character, narrative and plot developments of the serial. She finds the more positive elements in the articulation of the social realist genre in *Coronation Street* with other, more 'open' genres that do not require the illusion of synonymity with life – the production of the response, 'life's like that'. I would want to extend her argument by suggesting that *all* texts are (relatively) open, including those that inhabit one or another of the varieties of realism.

While it is true that the typical realist narrative begins with a disturbance of the class or patriarchal order, and works through its consequences in such a way that order is restored, yet typically more is thrown into play in the initial disturbance than is ever resolved at the end. *Coronation Street* is amply supplied with the strong, middle-aged women characters which the conventions of soap opera seem to require. To retain their dramatic interest, these women must remain independent. Bill Podmore, the current producer of the programme, has remarked in connection with Rita's marriage to Len Fairclough, that marriage easily diminishes a character, and it was no surprise to find, eighteen short months later, that Len and Rita's marriage was under threat, and Rita had left home. However such a 'disturbance' will be resolved, whether by Rita (temporarily) returning to Len or, alternatively, to the marriage market for a lover or husband, the acknowledgment of the difficulty of maintaining the norms of romantic love and marriage still stands, and is reaffirmed again and again in the serial. In this particular case indeed it is difficult to know what constitutes order and what disturbance. In a sense, the conventions of the genre are such that the normal order of things in *Coronation Street* is precisely that of broken marriages, temporary liaisons, availability for 'lasting' romantic love which in fact never lasts. This order, the reverse of the patriarchal norm, is in a sense interrupted by the marriages and 'happy family' interludes, rather than vice-versa. The breakdown of Rita and Len's marriage, if it occurs, will be a resolution of the problem which Podmore has created in marrying them in the first place.

Coronation Street offers its women viewers certain 'structures of feeling' which are prevalent in our society, and which are only partially recognised in the normative patriarchal order. It offers women a validation and celebration of those interests and concerns which are seen as properly theirs within the social world they inhabit. Soap opera may be the opium of masses of women, but like religion, it may also be, if not 'the sign of the oppressed', yet a context in which women can ambiguously express *both* good-humoured acceptance of their oppression *and* recognition of that oppression, and some equally good-humoured protest against it. In the words of Sheila Rowbotham, it is an expression and celebration of the way in which:

> . . . women have resolutely manoeuvred for a better position within the general context of subordination – by shifting for themselves, turning the tables, ruling the roost, wearing the trousers, hen-pecking, gossiping, hustling, or (in the words of a woman I once overheard) just 'going drip drip at him' (Rowbotham, 1979).

No wonder men dislike it!

This validation and celebration is, it is true, offered within a genre which is ghettoised and despised by media workers, intellectuals, and men generally. The more prestigious products which media specialists prefer to focus upon in 'serious' discussions of television include documentaries, news, drama documentaries, plays, current affairs programmes, but never 'women's' programmes. This universal denigration lingers even among critics who have extended their interests to popular 'male' genres such as the Western. A recent National Film Theatre programme included the following comment on the television Western, *Bonanza*: 'From 1959-1963 *Bonanza* enjoyed phenomenal success, changing slowly from "Western" to "soap opera" as patriarch Lorne Greene and sons Michael Landin, Dan Blocker and . . . Pernell Roberts defended their Ponderosa ranch from hazard, and *tamed the wildness of the genre* . . .' (my emphasis) (NFT Programme Booklet, Oct-Nov. 1979). Yet within this almost universal denigration, soap opera does provide the pleasures of validation, and of self-assertion, which must surely go some way to accounting for its lasting popularity with women.

There are of course precedents for strong women characters within the available stereotypes developed and used in other popular genres, for example the great female stars of Hollywood in the 30s and 40s. But the images developed in the long-running serial add a new dimension, partly because the discrete plots of 90-minute movies do not allow the same scope for developing characters whose final return to the patriarchal order in the formal closures of the narrative is impeded by the resonances which accumulate around them and make them partially unrecuperable.* *Coronation Street* has been running for twenty years. Many characters have come and gone in that period, but a substantial number have remained. They have grown older with the serial, although fictional age does not necessarily

---

* Richard Dyer's analysis suggests, however, that similar resonances may be accumulated around the star herself rather than the character she plays in any given film. See R. Dyer, *Stars,* BFI, London 1979.

keep pace with the duration of the programme.

One source of pleasure for middle-aged housewives watching *Coronation Street*, who themselves, in this role, are stereotypically desexualised within an ageist and sexist culture, must surely be its sexualisation of the middle-aged, the ordinary, the housewife. Interestingly, the group of older women – Elsie, Bet, Rita – who play this role are far more compelling in it than their younger counterparts. That this is not just a personal judgment is perhaps confirmed by the recent decision to chop Suzie and Steve from the programme. The younger women, Suzie and Gail, are more interesting in their relationships with older women such as Elsie than they are in their more obvious place as centres of romantic intrigue.

Because the demands of soap opera require strong independent women, and because these qualities are more readily reconciled with experience and a degree of financial independence, the women protagonists are not only typically middle-aged, but also tend to work outside the home as well as within it. Again, this kind of representation presents no particular difficulties in terms of the dominant ideology, as Jordan has shown, yet this is still an important extension of the range of imagery which is offered to women within popular forms, and as such, is welcome.

Popular culture, then, like common sense, is contradictory and ambiguous when related to the politics of class and sex. It might be thought that this is to say no more than has already been said in the 'cracks and fissures' approach, for instance that of *Cahiers,* referred to above. But the oppositional valences of popular culture are not treasure buried in the depth of the text, and recoverable only with the aid of the right kinds of readings which are the exclusive preserve of a highly educated élite. They are very much more on the surface of the text, part of the staple pleasures which popular culture affords its audience. It is because these utopian and oppositional elements of popular culture – those elements which express the hopes, fears, wishes and simple refusals of the dominated – are *not* marginal but defining elements which are essential to the whole meaning and appeal of popular entertainment, that work in and on these forms, by media workers as well as critics, is of interest and importance.

THE LIBRARY
GUILDFORD COLLEGE
52
of Further and higher Education

RICHARD PATERSON

The Production Context
of *Coronation Street*

This essay is concerned with the institutional and organisational context of
the production of *Coronation Street* by Granada Television's Manchester
studios. Its perspective is that the complex structure of a commercial broadcasting organisation, subject to both legislative and IBA pressures, has to be
understood when analysing the conditions of existence of its programme
production.

The particular features of *Coronation Street* stem from its continuous
production, twice weekly since December 1960, which necessitated the
setting up of a *Coronation Street* office. Analysis of this office's operation and
the routine of production enables us to understand the constraints affecting
continuous serials – constraints which are both technical and to do with
time. This can be compared with the production of other television drama,
such as Thames Television's series *Hazell* and the Euston Films production
of *The Sweeney*, to indicate some of the differences between the problems
and their resolution within serial drama and series drama. Further, the
implications for both the narrative development and significational
strategy* of series and serial dramas derive from different technical problems and from placement in the television schedule. *Coronation Street* has
been placed at 7.30 on Monday and Wednesday evenings for most of its
existence, and this has ramifications in terms of narrative and audience
construction, returning the analysis to the institutional context of British
television and the circulation of television as a commodity. This essay seeks
to elucidate these factors in the production of *Coronation Street* in order to
contextualise the detailed analyses of other essays in this book. Furthermore, it is the contention of this essay that aesthetic and ideological analyses
must take account of these influences on significational strategies.

1. GRANADA TELEVISION

Coronation Street is produced by Granada Television, a subsidiary of the
Granada Group Ltd. In addition to the IBA television contract it holds for
Lancashire and surrounding areas, the Group lists its principal activities as:
television set rental, property investment and development, insurance and

---

* By this I mean the particular ways in which all the signs (both visual and aural) are used to create
meaning in the narrative.

life assurance, bingo social clubs and cinemas, motorway services, book publishing and music publishing (*Directors' Report* no. 45, p. 1). In 1979 the Group profit was £39 million on a turnover of £277.5 million, with the turnover of the television operation being £65.5 million, contributing 16.3% of the profits. The major profit earner in the Group's 1979 activities was television rental, which contributed 61.9% of the profits.

Comparison with Group activities in 1967 shows a significant change in the proportion of turnover and profit attributable to the television and television rental operations. In 1967 the turnover of the Group totalled £33.1 million (television £20 million), with a Group profit of £4.6 million of which the television operation contributed 87.7% and television rentals only 6.5%. Granada lost the Yorkshire area from its franchise in 1968, which accounts for some loss of revenue from television, but the figures indicate a major diversification of Group activities out of the insecurity of limited tenure television franchise operations and into a wide field of other activities, dominated by television rentals. This diversification – the building up of Granada as a media conglomerate – has been capitalised on the profits accrued in the 60s from the TV franchise.

Granada's original business was luxury cinemas, out of which the initial television operation was a major diversification. Granada commenced transmission in Lancashire on 3 May 1956 and in Yorkshire in November 1956; but, in common with the other early operators, very quickly encountered major financial difficulties:

> In spite of the possibility of limited cost sharing after ATV's Midland station opened in February 1956, Associated Rediffusion and ATV began to wonder how much more money their boards and shareholders would consent to pour into this bottomless well (Black, 1972, pp. 96-7).

> Granada . . . lost £176,928 by 30 April 1957, when its financial year ended (Seglow, 1978, p. 93).

In July 1956 Bernstein of Granada and Spencer Wills of Associated Rediffusion signed an agreement whereby Rediffusion provided 85% of Granada's programmes, in consideration of which Granada undertook to pay Associated Rediffusion 'the whole of its net annual advertising revenue, less an agreed proportion' (Black 1972, p. 103). The risks of Granada's television operation were thus taken over by Associated Rediffusion, and up to the termination of the agreement four years later this resulted in a payment by Granada to Associated Rediffusion of £8,044,238. Thus the initial years of super profits in Independent Television (after 1958) were in large part denied Granada Television, which also had to provide only 15% of its own programmes up to 1960. *Coronation Street* was thus part of a necessary expansion of programme-making by Granada in 1960. Interestingly, this expansion took a radical innovatory form for British television, explainable in part by the nature of the company.

The major shareholder in Granada was, and continues to be, the Bernstein family, which has a tradition of support for the Labour Party. Indeed Sidney Bernstein (until recently chairman of the Granada Group) guaranteed the bank loan of the fledgling Association of Cinematograph Technicians (now the ACTT) in 1935 (Chanan, 1976, p. 31).

Granada Television is one of the five network companies within the IBA franchise structure (the others are, currently, Thames, ATV, Yorkshire and London Weekend) charged with providing programmes for network transmission on Independent Television. IBA franchises are also given to regional companies, whose main function is the provision of programmes for their own areas. Thus within a region programmes come partly from these regional companies and partly from the network companies. Granada's contribution to network programmes is determined by their share of the net advertising revenue, after levy, earned by the entire network (Annan Report 1977, p. 173), and the allocation of responsibility for programmes is worked out by the Programme Controllers Group of the ITCA (consisting of the programme controllers of the five network companies, plus the IBA Director of Television and the Director of the Network Programme Secretariat). One of the major, and continuing, contributions to the network from Granada has been *Coronation Street*, which has aggregated high audience ratings for most of its history. In addition to its profitability (in terms of generating advertising) in Britain, the programme has been sold to many foreign broadcasting stations, while spin-offs have included a series of books (published by Mayflower, a Granada subsidiary) on the early years of the programme: *Coronation Street: Early Days*; *Trouble at the Rovers*; and *Elsie Tanner Fights Back*, all by H.V. Kershaw. Coverage of the 'stars' of the serial in the popular press is wide and continuing, and the programme makes an important contribution to British popular culture, with a clearly enormous and devoted following.

Granada Television had a reputation for 'radicalism' and innovation in programme production (*World in Action, Sam, Reports Action*) up to the early 70s, and has also established its own regional identity through its network and local output. Its reputation for reflecting its regional base is due in part to the realism of *Coronation Street*. This acts as an important legitimation of the company's claim to remain the contractor for this area, since the IBA has a particular liking for programmes that reflect a regional identity. *Coronation Street* also achieves large audiences in Granada's franchise area and consequent high advertising revenue expectations; it almost invariably tops the ratings in the North-west.

The importance of ratings success is evident (cf. Alvarado and Buscombe, *Hazell*, 1978, p. 28). Bill Podmore's taking over as producer of *Coronation Street* in 1975 from Susi Hush is an illustration of the pressures to which 'popular' programmes are subject. In this case they became public because of Granada's obvious disquiet at the downturn in ratings with the introduction of 'serious' issues. The company's central concern was commercial, and

55

only aesthetic inasmuch as that was seen to determine the ratings.* Bill Podmore's reputation as a producer of comedy (e.g. *My Brother's Keeper, Nearest and Dearest*) signalled a change in direction away from 'drama' and a quest for humour and entertainment, and within two years the programme had re-established itself as a ratings success. The rest of the collective authorship (storyline writers, script writers) remained virtually unchanged over this period.

2. THE STREET

Coronation Street was first broadcast at 7 p.m. on Friday 9 December 1960. This was the first of twelve episodes written by Tony Warren, the programme's creator; and, as Pat Phoenix has written, the programme 'quickly established itself as a firm favourite with viewers in the North ... From March 1961, it was shown in other parts of the country where it proved equally popular'. The early social realism of the serial, redolent of late 50s British films, and its continuation of a tradition in TV drama documentaries of that period of 'recreating reality' (Scannel, 1979, p. 102), has in part been modified by the early standardisation of production, the accumulative connotations of the narrative space and the imperatives of the continuous serial form.

In the early days, Friday's episode was transmitted live and was immediately followed by a tele-recording of the Monday episode – that is, the two episodes were recorded in one session. Even after the introduction of VTR, the two programmes were recorded as a continuous performance until 1974. The production of the programme in colour began in 1969. These different technical factors have evident significational importance. Thus continuous performance as opposed to the rehearse-record-edit method used now (see below) caused problems of narrative construction because of the difficulties of time lapse/costume change; while recording in colour has certain ideological implications (cf. E. Buscombe on sound and colour in film, *Jump Cut* no. 17).

---

*The JICTAR national ratings show that in 1975 *Coronation Street* had fallen from its usual position as one of the top ten audience pullers. Thus in the week ending Sunday 19 October 1975, the Monday episode was 12th in the weekly ratings with an estimated audience of 7.30 million homes, and the Wednesday episode 20th with 6.35 million homes viewing. However by the week ending Sunday 15 October 1978 the Monday episode was 1st in JICTAR national ratings, and the Wednesday episode 7th, with an estimated 17.80 million and 15.05 million individual viewers respectively. These 'national' figures conceal regional differences in the programme's popularity and also don't indicate the demographic breakdown of the audience. While these in themselves could form the basis of another paper, it is possible to discern broad trends in the change of audience composition between 1975 and 1980, from the figures which JICTAR supply to their subscribers. In the North-west (Granadaland) there was an increase in the proportion of available homes tuned in, with a small increase in the proportion of housewives and women viewing (they are classified separately), a static but quite high male viewership, but a substantial increase in the child audience.

A more important determinant of signification in all its aspects is the regularisation of production from the *Coronation Street* office. Though this has been modified in minor ways over the years, it has become a continuing, constraining and in part determining feature of significational and narrative possibilities. If the production of *Coronation Street* is compared to that of *Hazell*, both are seen to have an all-powerful producer, a script editor, an original creator, plus a small group of writers and itinerant directors – that is, an office serviced by specialised staff. The early difficulties of a series like *Hazell*, as described by Alvarado and Buscombe – the search for a style, the compromises, the problems of a new production – are of course no longer a part of the production of *Coronation Street*.

The *Coronation Street* office acts with virtual autonomy, although the producer is formally responsible to the Head of Drama. Granada Television's organisational structure has allowed some cross-fertilisation between departments through the transference of personnel (cf. Goldie 1977, p. 210, on the importance of this interaction in the genesis of *Tonight*). Many directors have been trained on *Coronation Street*, and indeed the present Granada Programme Controller, Mike Scott, was a director on the early episodes. In addition to the overall producer, the office consists of a programme planner (with responsibility for the logistics of production), two storyline writers, a script editor, a biographical record keeper, and secretarial staff. At any one time three directors, with production assistants, working on various stages of the production of a pair of episodes, will be attached to the office. However, in common with the practice in other companies, cameramen, technicians and other personnel are not allocated permanently to the serial (cf. Alvarado and Buscombe 1978, p. 112).

Every three weeks a story conference is convened to make decisions about the narrative progression of a further six episodes, within the broader framework of a long-term conference held periodically to map out future directions. In attendance at the story conference are the producer, the series planner, the storyline writers and a number of script writers.* Plot developments for a three-week period are discussed and proceedings and decisions minuted. The storyline writers then produce the outlines of six episodes based on the decisions of the conference, and these are allocated to suitable writers. Certain writers have established reputations for types of storyline, and this, together with availability, is used as a basis for allocating episodes. Additionally, some writers are used to handle important narrative moments – a small core group whose knowledge and 'understanding' of the programme has been acquired over a long period of association. Each writer is contracted for a set number of scripts over a set period.

The storyline writers' outline indicates which members of the cast are available, who has been written out or is on holiday, and the sets allocated

---

* Cf. 'How the backroom boys kept Stan Ogden out of jail', *TV Times*, Vol. 85, No. 46, 4 November 1976, p. 30.

for use in the episode. The plot is broken down into scenes which broadly detail the action, characters involved and set in use. Before the writers start work on the script, a commissioning conference is convened at which the producer, series planner and six writers finalise details of the stories, ensuring that the episodes mesh into a consistent narrative. From the story outline the writer must develop a 26-minute script, utilising all the narrative points though not necessarily following slavishly the ordering of points or dramatic emphases.

For *Crossroads*, on the other hand, there are 'five or six story lines running at the same time, so that each of [the] writers works on his own story, with his own characters, without concerning himself as to what is happening to the rest of the *Crossroads* folk . . . individual segments which when pieced together make up the whole programme' (Gordon, 1975, p. 41). Currently a small team of writers is credited on *Crossroads*, and the practice on *Coronation Street* of using a cohering author (no matter how dubious his or her authorship) is still not employed.

Series formats too are fairly rigid. However, there is a greater leeway allowed to the writer because of the self-contained nature of each episode. There are usually less restrictions in the production timetable and often a greater freedom with production techniques (thus the freedom felt by *The Sweeney* production staff in the use of film rather than video for recording) when compared with the tight limitations of serial production.

Coronation Street's scripts are delivered in sequence over a two-three week period. Each episode is the collective product of conference, storyline writers and script writer – with the script writer credited as author. Coherence with preceding narrative detail, character development, continuity between scripts and maintenance of the 'style' of *Coronation Street* is ensured by the script editor. Thus no out of place characterisation is possible, and any biographical details in question are referred to the *Street*'s biographer. As Christine Geraghty points out, each episode must attempt to maintain audience interest to ensure repeat viewing, while not progressing too fast so as not to alienate the occasional viewer. A poser – what Geraghty calls the 'cliffhanger device' – is included at the end of each episode, and to a lesser extent before the advertising break in the middle of each episode, in the attempt to ensure repeat viewing.

After passing the script editor, each pair of episodes is allocated to a director, who has responsibility for one week's output. The directors employed tend to be staff members, although it is sometimes necessary to employ freelance workers. Each director is given three weeks to bring the scripts into recorded episode form. The first task is the preparation of a camera script – indicating shot type and camera use, camera deployment in sets etc., for each scene. Set deployment in the studio has to be mapped out. Rehearsal and recording take place in the third week. Monday is used for the recording of any outside scenes – usually on electronic cameras in the Street set near the Manchester studios, although occasionally using film cameras in other parts of Manchester; while Tuesday and Wednesday are taken up with rehearsals. Studio recording of the two episodes is done on Thursday afternoon and all day Friday, moving from set to set rehearsing then recording each scene on electronic cameras. On some occasions several takes are necessary, but the restrictions of time deter unnecessary delay. Technical problems or actor fallibility were more of a hazard when the episode was recorded in one continuous take. The final takes for each scene are edited together in half a day with the director in the week after the recording. The episodes are transmitted two weeks later.

Actor/actress availability for each episode depends mainly on plot requirement. However, an additional constraint is imposed by the fact that their contracts specify appearance in a certain number of episodes over a specified time (the storyline writers keep statistics on appearances), while a character's prolonged absence from the Street, or lack of central plot elements in which characters are involved, may create problems of narrative realism.

Restricted studio space and lack of time for changes during the two days of recording limits the number of sets available for each pair of episodes (generally there are five sets available). However, as will be argued below, this is an important significational factor in continuous serial production, which is further determined by the need to maintain an understandable mythic space.

Coronation Street is, then, an important part of the output from Granada's Manchester studios. The assured use each week of high capital cost equipment and studio facilities (below the line costs) is an important factor in a broadcasting company's resource use. Minimal above the line costs (little expenditure on new sets, location shooting, etc.) enable Granada to provide a very popular production for the ITV network at low cost, with high returns to itself and the other commercial companies from advertising revenue at peak viewing time. This allows for more innovative and expensive programme production, as well as further diversification of the Granada Group. At the same time *Coronation Street*'s success satisfies the IBA's concern for 'regionalism' in production, which is a positive factor when the Authority considers franchise renewals.

3. SERIES DRAMA AND SERIAL DRAMA

Series and serial dramas are central elements of the output of British commercial television. As Goodhardt et al. point out, broadcasters believe audiences like repetition; organisationally it is prudent to cope with the enormous demand for programmes by using formulae; and – most important – commercial television requires a fairly stable and predictable audience (Goodhardt et al., 1975, p. 6). Scheduling is a fundamental determinant of form and content (Paterson, 1980), oriented to the notion (and reinforcement) of a family dynamic: that the domestic environment and patterns of living are related to the television schedule.

The serial and series are different products aimed at different markets using different organisations of the production routine. There are *some* similarities – collective production, the requirement for continuity of characters and places – but these are displaced by production values and by the construction of the programmes into schedules. That is, they are differentiated by the notion of how the aggregated family audience can be maximised at different times and by the suitability of the product for the different slots.

One approach to the difference of two serials – *Coronation Street* and *Crossroads*, for example – is to examine their position in the schedule and relate this to the IBA time-bands and a professional ideology of broadcasters. If we adopt this method the lack of a total coherence to the *Crossroads* narrative (for the reasons of multiple authorship outlined above) by offering multiple small segments in a serial stripped over three (previously four and five) nights each week at 6.35 or 5.15 p.m. (according to area) can be seen to fit into the professional ideology of a toddlers' truce, as well as the stipulations about time-bands and suitable programming made by the IBA. The toddlers' truce (cf. Goldie, 1977, p. 209) was based on the idea of no programme transmissions between 6.00 and 7.00 p.m. so that children could be put to bed. Its use is seen to necessitate programmes which consist of multiple short items that a non-static household is able to absorb selectively. That is, the belief that people will put the television on for programmes that do not require constant attention, whereas they would not for a long and involving narrative, was important to the genesis of *Tonight* (and its successor *Nationwide*), and can be seen to fit the *Crossroads* narrative structure. *Crossroads* can also be scheduled at earlier times because it fits the IBA stipulation about the need to cater for a very differentiated audience with a large proportion of children watching alone at either of its transmission times (see above). If this is compared to the audience expected to be watching at 7.30 – a static family audience with the mother present and central in determining channel selection, able to absorb a more coherent narrative, and a need to aggregate a large audience to induce high advertising expenditure – it is clear that the *Coronation Street* narrative fits these requirements. *Hazell* or *The Sweeney*, on the other hand, are both designed for the action series slot after 9.00 p.m. – programmes with greater dramatic licence because the responsibility for what children should watch is believed to lie with parents. Hence stipulations in the IBA *Television Programme Guidelines*: that programmes shown after 9.00 p.m. may be 'progressively less suitable (i.e. more adult) material'. After 9.00 p.m. there is an attempt to aggregate a different audience based on the 'adult'.

The placing of programmes in the schedule is an important factor of difference of television forms (and in television drama of the various subgroups: crime thrillers, family sagas, etc.). The series form and the narrative strategies utilised within it have been analysed by Phillip Drummond with reference to *The Sweeney* – a hermeneutic of detection, the necessity for the expulsion of the 'difference' asserted by the villain, within a series motif that includes the mythology of a perpetuity of characters, but with stories not flowing from one episode to the next. The narrative strategies of *Coronation Street* also sometimes rely on the expulsion of any difference (any threat to the integrity of the Street), but the narrative continuity is much more marked without, however, any definite or necessary resolution of the various hermeneutics – continuation does not require resolution (cf. the essays by Geraghty and by Paterson and Stewart). The progression of the narrative is limited by the need not to move on too rapidly. It was discovered in early soap opera production in the United States that too rapid narrative progression annoys an audience and disposes it not to follow. As Stedman says of the radio serial: '. . . on an average a housewife heard between two and three episodes of a given drama each week . . . The pace of the serials at no time bothered her as much as it did researchers and critics . . . Pace bothered the housewife only in one circumstance: when she missed a broadcast and something did happen' (Stedman, 1977, p. 275). This is further validated by work on audience behaviour by Goodhardt et al. which shows a low repeat-viewing pattern of successive series episodes so that 'for any extended series of episodes . . . almost no one sees all, or even nearly all, the different episodes' (op. cit., p. 126). In fact in April/May 1971 repeat viewing of *Coronation Street* by London housewives in successive weeks was high at 63% (the average for the programmes researched was 54%) (Goodhardt et al., 1975, p. 57).

Thus the consumption pattern of the programme is another prime determinant of narrative structure – a narrative slowness is necessitated, together with a pre-signalling of major dramatic events (and here the popular press can be used to ensure both a maximisation of audience and a prevention of annoyance at missing the major event – despite 'shocked' reactions of companies to story leaks), and a continuation of the explanation of events in the dialogue of ensuing episodes.

In addition to the importance of schedule placement in the circulation of the *Coronation Street* text, anchorage of the audience into a regular slot as part of the domestic routine, marketing and distribution of associated memorabilia, usually in the form of *TV Times* Souvenir Specials, further contribute to audience involvement. The persistent mythologisation of the 'place' in the narrative, and the circulation of myths about Street life, are reinforced. These elements are further elaborated in popular press coverage of key events.

'Publicity', be it events in the lives of the stars, or events in the Street narrative, reported by the press, is a key element in the moving forward of the maze of understanding of the viewer. Furthermore, Granada's publication of three novels based on the early years of the Street was presumably believed to be a potentially profitable enterprise – an assumed demand for archaeological detail.

Independent Television Publications has published four special souvenir publications on *Coronation Street*. The first (in 1967) dealt with the wedding of Elsie Tanner to the American Steve Tanner. Another wedding (that of Len and Rita) was commemorated by a souvenir in 1977. The other two marked the 1,000th episode in 1970 and the 2,000th in 1980. Independent Television Publications sell about half a million of each (including exports to those countries where *Coronation Street* is shown – for example, Australia) and they claim that the main market is with older people. If we examine two souvenir extras – 'There's a Wedding in the Street' and 'Coronation Street 2000' – we can see that they mainly consist of items which reiterate memory points for the Street; they are further elements in the maintenance of audience interest and commitment. Thus the ritual elements in a wedding are outlined within the ongoing narrative textuality – nodal points in the narrative allow a recapitulation of street history as well as a recasting of character. Hence in the souvenir issue for the wedding of Len and Rita, the biography of Len and Rita situates the history of their relationships with members of the opposite sex and recalls the previous Street weddings; key moments in the story. To engage the further interest of the viewer the wedding is prefigured (and a memory of it provided) by a selection from Rita's wedding album, with comments ascribed to her written alongside. The engagement with the mythic reality of the Street is repeated and circulated to Street 'fans', and the unification of the myths, the spreading out of the memory, all achieved across texts in different media, create repetition and effect reinforcement of the mode of serial consumption – a crucial specificity of continuity and circulation.

4. SIGNIFICATION IN THE CONTEXT OF PRODUCTION

Central to the understanding of a text is the analysis of its system of representation. However, it can be misleading simply to analyse appearances, or to attempt to transfer concepts employed to analyse one medium (such as a film) to the analysis of another (such as the television serial). As argued above, a central factor in the analysis of a television serial is its mode of reception. Though textual analysis does not itself deal with this area, what it can – and must – engage with is the signifying practices that are determined by the form and its conditions of production, separate from though related to the conditions of existence imposed by the reception mode.

The significational strategy of *Coronation Street* is bounded by significant constraints – place use (limited sets and the restricted narrative possibilities in a 'street'), camera strategy within the spaces used (the conventional shot strategy in the Rovers Return, for instance), a need to maintain the mythic realism of life in a northern street. The title shots and the theme music, opening and closing each episode, map off the street as a separate world; and the televisual construction of space has a central narrative function, which positions the spectator as a unified (and knowing) subject of vision

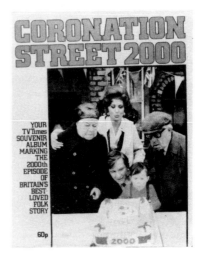

within that world. The sets, and the placing by the camera of the characters in relation to them, constitute spaces that prevalue the foregrounded dialogue – a complex audience-address, interweaving well known spaces and their accumulative value with the dialogue into a constant narrative renewal. These places compensate for the irregular viewing pattern of audience members – nothing is too unexpected, no matter how the dialogue and plot develop.

The centrality of place (and the space within it, realised through camerawork) is a product of the determinations of serialisation. In *Coronation Street*, the principal example of the importance of place is the Rovers Return. Here the narrative is made coherent and almost all narrative strands are discussed in this main place of exchange in the Street. At the same time there is a continuous creation of character-text for each character – a biography that has a past and a future within the mythic reality – through a specific televisual signification, meshing performance, kinesis and positioning for camera. For in *Coronation Street* the emphasis is on a group of characters living in a bounded milieu (and in this respect we can compare *Coronation Street* with a series such as *Hazell*, which is focused on one central character moving through a number of constantly changing locations), but this is also contained by the limitations of studio production.

Studio production restricts the size of sets and the number of sets available in any episode. The pre-existing pressure of the serial concept toward an ideology of 'family and community' life in a northern street (no matter how difficult this becomes because of personnel changes) cannot easily be changed to deal, for example, with the central social and economic contradictions of capital and labour in the workplace. It is difficult, if not impossible, to incorporate the industrial situation, with the necessary large sets, into restricted studio space. Narrative progression is oriented to dialogue and action within the home or the place of exchange (the shop, the pub). When industrial problems are introduced they are inevitably trivialised into the spaces available, reinforcing an unsympathetic treatment of the Labour movement. This can account in part for the television serial concentration on the situation of the petit bourgeois family. But of course radio serials of the 30s and 40s in the USA also concentrated on the domestic to the exclusion of the industrial, albeit without the problems of televisual signification (cf. Edmondson and Rounds, 1973, p. 18).

The style of *Coronation Street* includes a conventionality of camerawork. The particular rhetoric of the shot strategy coheres with the performance of actresses and actors in the realisation of the narrative. Normal camera strategy uses two or three cameras on each set, and only a limited vocabulary of shots is utilised. Generally group shots, 2-shots or 3-shots are used (in medium to medium close-up), with emphasis achieved through the medium close-up or close-up of a single character (usually in shot reverse-shot sequence). Sometimes a developing shot is used with the camera panning to follow the action. In an early episode there is a tracking shot, though this is

Fig. 2

never used in current production. Shots concentrate on characters, and only very seldom are inanimate objects viewed alone, and then for emphasis of some point of the dialogue (e.g. the photo of Jack Walker, redolent with the mythic history of the Street). The cutting between shots is almost invariably motivated by dialogue. Camera strategy *can* be used, though it is unusual, to provide dramatic emphases, such is the conventionality of the normal shot repertoire. Thus in the episode where Bet learns of the death of her son in a car accident (a son she has never known) angled shots and close-ups are used to emphasise the high drama (see Fig. 2).

What has been argued in this section is that camera strategy, set restrictions and conventionalised use of space, together with the limitations of time and technical constraints, impose a certain stylistic rhetoric on the serial. These determinations of the production context are central elements in the

65

construction of the serial-text, and must be taken into account in elaborations of the coded text – i.e. in our understanding of the programme. The technical constraints and conventionalised strategies are as important as those of the schedule or of cultural codes. But there is an overdetermination of the form that is reflected in part in Susi Hush's comment in 1974 that 'it will never get to what I want to see. It's got a reality of its own and you can't pre-empt it'.

MARION JORDAN

Character Types and the Individual

Two of the articles in this monograph ('The Continuous Serial – a Definition' and 'Realism and Convention') suggest ways in which the characters in
Coronation Street may be grouped. In an attempt to help thinking and
discussion on the subject we include here as *aide-mémoire* a directory of
fictional biographies and narrative appearances (compiled with the help of
Coronation Street's archivist, Eric Rosser) of selected characters, grouped
under the kinds of heading suggested in these two essays. The primary
grouping is by means of status position held (in the manner suggested in
Christine Geraghty's paper). These may change, however, from year to year
and it is impossible to establish such positions with complete constancy. The
principle adopted here is to include characters under the position which
they occupy most frequently, even if they are currently otherwise designated. No attempt is made to resolve the apparent contradictions which
emerge. Indeed, one of the points of the exercise is to enable viewers to
check on such contentions as the claim in 'Realism and Convention' that the
apparent settling-for-life is only illusorily permanent. These position
groupings may also help in the estimation of the extent to which *Coronation
Street* departs from the convention of other works of the type, for example in
its use of middle-aged women as a prime source of romantic involvement.

   Where the primary group is large sub-sets are suggested which accord
with the social types proposed in 'The Continuous Serial'. Again the apparent paradoxes which emerge (as, for example, the listing of a sub-set
'Spinsterly Types' in the group 'Marriageable Women' or the inclusion of a
crustily confirmed bachelor – in fact a widower – of 85 among the marriageable men) are included without attempt at resolution, to enable viewers to
test for themselves such contentions as the claim in 'Realism and Convention' that the generic demand for stereotyping (supposedly a flexible proce-
dure) is so prescriptive as often to override the facts (supposedly inflexible)
of position-holding.

   We have no wish to suggest that the grouping adopted here is the only
possible one. Readers/viewers may find it interesting to try out alternative
groupings for themselves.

   Within the groups suggested the listing is alphabetical. Since performers
clearly influence strongly the nature of the roles they play, the names of the
actors concerned are included in brackets immediately after the name of the
role.

Minnie Caldwell (Margot Bryant), b.1900, widowed 1935, no children.
Minnie Caldwell stood alongside Ena Sharples from the first as a quasi-grandmother. She has always been softer than Ena, however, and her kindness was often abused in the early days. She took in Eddie Yeats when he first came to Coronation Street (in place of another rogue). She left Coronation Street (since the actress who played the part is too old to return) to act as housekeeper to a wealthy old flame.

Martha Longhurst (Lynne Carole), b.1899, m.1919, widowed 1946, d.1964, daughter Lily 1925, son Harold 1926.
Martha used to stand (or more commonly sit in The Rovers Return) along-side Minnie and Ena as a representative of an already aging indigenous group. She died of a heart attack in The Rovers in 1964.

Ena Sharples (Violet Carson), b.1889, m.1920, widowed 1937, daughters Madge 1922 (gone abroad), Vera 1927 (d.1967).
Mrs Sharples lives in the Community Centre flat. She has had a hard life, working in the mill in the mornings from the age of eight, and attending Factory School in the afternoons. Though past retiring age when the programme started she has always worked as resident caretaker, first at the Glad Tidings Mission, then at the Coronation Street Community Centre. She is on the whole (unlike Minnie Caldwell) more given to good advice, often caustically expressed, than to good works, and consistently deplores the decline in standards. Her devotion to 'the community' is often signalled by her playing of the piano for community singing.

Betty Turpin (Betty Driver), b.1920, m.1949, widowed 1974, son Gordon Clegg.
Betty Turpin is younger than the other figures in this section, and is only recently graduating to the status of grandmother figure, and still, of course, unable to pass the only rigorous test – pre- or post-World War I. At least until 1975 she was still being used for marriage plots. She is a native of Manchester, who returned with her husband, a policeman, after twenty years in Birmingham to stay with her sister Maggie Clegg, who at that time was a partner in the corner shop. She became a barmaid at The Rovers Return in 1969. She was originally presented as a bossy older sister who quarrelled with Maggie when Maggie forestalled her getting a part share in the shop. With the years she has mellowed and become impeccably respectable, despite the revelation to the community in 1974 that Gordon Clegg, who had been brought up by Maggie, was actually Betty's illegitimate son. She is trusted, though bossed, by Annie Walker, who tries to give her dignity by addressing her as Elizabeth, and she looks on the world with a sense of bemused kindness.

Annie Walker (Doris Speed), b.1909, m. Jack Walker, widowed 1970, son Billy 1938, daughter Joan 1940.

Landlady of The Rovers Return, Coronation Street. Mrs Walker's only education was at the local council school in Clitheroe, and she started work at the cotton mill. She keeps both these facts fairly well hidden, however, preferring the social image of the description of herself as a Beaumont of Clitheroe. Certainly she considers herself as the only person in the street who is the educational equal of Ken Barlow, and is confident that she is socially a cut above everyone else. If she deceives Coronation Street about her origins she deceives herself about her children. Her daughter Joan, who lives in Derby, is selfish and grasping, and her son Billy has both stolen from her and deceived her, yet both remain the apple of her eye, and she never ceases to boast of them. When Alf Roberts was Mayor in 1973 she was his Mayoress, and she soon after bought a Rover car as a suitable adjunct to her status. Fred is occasionally used to chauffeur her in this on occasions like the meetings of the Lady Victuallers' Association.

MARRIAGEABLE WOMEN

(a) Mature, sexy women

Rita Fairclough (Barbara Knox), *née* Littlewood, b.1932, m. Len Fairclough 1977.

Stage-struck from childhood, Rita is a former nightclub dancer and singer (still making occasional appearances) who never quite made it. She is now officially 48 and was installed as manageress in The Kabin by Len Fairclough in 1973. In the course of her appearance in the programme she has had, or been suspected of having, affairs of varying permanence with Dennis Tanner, Harry Bates (passing as his wife for some years, and finally leaving after being beaten up when suspected of having an affair with Len), Ken Barlow, Len Fairclough, and her nightclub employer. She married Len Fairclough in 1977 after a romantically last-minute (airport) renunciation of the bright lights of a nightclub in Tenerife. She is currently a respectable, though hot-tempered, wife, but is from time to time suspected (as when on holiday with Bet) of other liaisons.

Bet Lynch (Julie Goodyear), b.1940.

Bet is the stereotypical barmaid – sexy (at least as seen above the bar), sharp, cynical, yet wildly romantic at heart and always a sucker for a sob-story from outsiders. Her past difficulties include being the child of a broken home (her father left when she was 6 months old) and having an illegitimate baby at 16 which her mother forced her to have adopted. When she heard of the death of this unknown son in 1974 she prepared to attempt suicide in despair at the pointlessness of her life, and was saved only by the intervention of Eddie Yeats. She has had affairs with a lorry-driver (twice), Billy Walker, a County footballer, Len Fairclough, Mike Baldwin, all ne'er-do-wells of a kind who have all managed to convince her, for however short a time, that they were offering her lasting affection. She remains a lone (and lonely) figure, the only truly vulnerable inhabitant, despised as common by Annie Walker (who cannot bear the implication of the vulgar inherent in the name 'Bet' and who therefore addresses her as Betty) but on the whole valued by the other inhabitants.

Audrey Potter (Sue Nicholls)
Audrey Potter is a good-time girl who entered the programme recently as the mother of Gail, who was born illegitimately in 1958. She is not married, but there is a suggestion of a series of resident lovers. She is currently a source of embarrassment to Gail as flamboyantly common and sexually promiscuous.

Elsie Tanner (Pat Phoenix), *née* Grimshaw, b.1923; m.(1) Arnold Tanner 1939, divorced 1961, daughter Linda 1940 (sons Paul 1961, Martin 1964), son Dennis 1942; m.(2) Steve (M/Sgt. US Army, a former war-time sweetheart) 1967, separated almost immediately, died 1968; m.(3) Alan Howard 1970, divorced 1978, reverted to the name of Tanner.
Elsie Tanner has been in the programme from its inception. She has had innumerable affairs in this time, the most persistent being a running battle with Len Fairclough, who has proposed twice. Her *amours* have included a Chief Petty Officer, an art teacher, a club-owner, a local bookie, and most recently a glib-tongued chauffeur, Ron Mather, with whom she moved briefly to Torquay as housekeeper-chauffeur combination. She returned to her home at 11 Coronation Street on Christmas Eve 1979, somewhat cross that her employer had tried to take liberties with her, and furious that Ron was willing to tolerate this in order to keep his job. Elsie has had a number of lower managerial jobs, working variously in three gown shops, a laun-derette, a flower-shop, a warehouse, a café, and as supervisor at Baldwin's factory. Something of a slut in the early days of the programme, she is now invariably well turned out. She has a sharp tongue and a quick temper but despite her readiness to stand up for herself and her apparently hard-boiled attitude she has often shown great kindness. Her greatest trial has been her son Dennis, who has always been a bad lot.

Renee Roberts (Madge Hindle), *née* Bradshaw, b.1943, m. Alf Roberts 1978, died in car crash 1980.
Renee, like Mavis Riley, is a native of Weatherfield who moved away with her parents and decided to return when independent. Her opportunity came when the corner shop was up for sale in 1976. She bought the shop with the aid of a bank loan and made a go of it, standing up to old-timers like Hilda Ogden by refusing her credit, and taking on (and beating) Annie Walker by getting an off-licence for the sale of wine in her shop. She had a long-standing affair with a merchant sailor, Harry McLean, but they

70

decided that he did not fit into the street and he returned to sea. Renee married Alf Roberts in 1978 after protracted efforts to get him to pop the question. She was killed in a car crash in 1980 while receiving driving instruction from Alf.

(b) Spinsterly types
Emily Bishop (Eileen Derbyshire), *née* Nugent, b.1929, m. Ernest Bishop 1972, widowed 1978.
Emily Bishop, who lives at No. 3 Coronation Street, represents the middle-classes there, speaking Standard English to the manner born (Emily's father was a regimental sergeant-major in the Indian Army) and (with her remarkably similar husband in earlier days) earning either mockery or a pitying respect for the kindnesses prompted by her middle-class social conscience. Emily is a regular churchgoer and inveterate do-gooder, providing a home for Deirdre and the baby when Ray left, ensuring that Mavis does not spend Christmas alone. The role is often played in such a way as to suggest that Emily had been married many years, and the childlessness of the marriage is wistfully mourned, with perhaps a hint that such a bloodless couple could hardly expect to generate children. In fact, she was not married until she was nearly 43. Despite her essentially asexual presentation she was the lead in many early courtship episodes, coming near to marrying her boss at Gamma Garments, saved from marriage with the vicar only by a realisation that he was not firm enough in his beliefs, following up introductions from a marriage bureau without any success, and having a wildly romantic affair with a Hungarian building-site worker, with whom she left the district only to return alone three weeks later, disappointed that he feared to settle down but enriched with a new understanding of life. Since Ernest's dramatic death at the hands of robbers raiding Mike Baldwin's office she has already been the focus of another romantic affair with Arnold Swain, who married her bigamously in 1980 and from whom she separated almost immediately when the bigamy was revealed.

Mavis Riley (Thelma Barlow), b.1937.
Mavis is presented as a former school-friend of Emily Bishop despite the slight discrepancy in their ages, and shares many of her characteristics, being equally religious, and almost equally 'used' by others, though she is rather more petulantly resentful of such selfishness than is Emily. The cumulative factual record of her many (all disappointing) affairs looks odd beside her consistently tongue-tied response to male company and her embarrassment at any suggestion of sexuality. She came to work at The Kabin in 1972 quite specifically because she was hoping for a proposal from Jerry Booth, and left when she discovered that he had been divorced. She returned later to work first as a vet's receptionist, then at the corner shop, and eventually to be reinstated at The Kabin. Always in wan pursuit of marriage, she tried persistently for Jerry Booth until he told her he was still

l to r: Deirdre Langton, Bette Turpin, Hilda Ogden, Emily Bishop, Bet Lynch, Annie Walker, Rita Fairclough

in love with an old flame, came almost to the altar in 1975 with a Spanish immigrant only to find that he was marrying her in order to get a work permit, failed to gain anything except an evening with Ken Barlow from a dating service, hoped for results from an eminently suitable RSPCA visitor who backed out without any reason being given. She has an on-off relationship with a sales representative, Derek Wilton, who is as shy physically as Mavis herself. She went so far as to put down a deposit on a house but then discovered that Derek was fonder of his mother than of her.

(c) Young women
Gail Tilsley (Helen Worth), *née* Potter, b.1958, m. Brian Tilsley 1979, son 1980.
Gail is not an adolescent in years but is consistently treated as such. She joined the programme in 1974 when she came to work in Weatherfield and moved into digs with her friend Tricia at Elsie Tanner's. She had an affair with a man of 35 and was horrified to be cited in a divorce case. She returned after this to the image of the adolescent girl looking for giggly dates along with her new friend and fellow-lodger, Suzie Birchall, to whom she played second fiddle. She and Brian have managed to get a mortgage for a house

l to r: Minnie Caldwell, Annie Walker, Len Fairclough, Elsie Tanner, Jack Walker

Dennis and Elsie Tanner

on a new estate. She helped *Coronation Street* through a difficult New Year's Eve by almost having her baby in The Rovers Return.

Suzie Birchall (Cheryl Murray), b.1958.
Suzie is a product of a broken home who came to Coronation Street in 1976 looking for work. She worked in different capacities for Mike Baldwin and joined Gail Potter as a lodger at Elsie Tanner's. She is always headstrong, often misguided. Though the programme presented with approval her refusal to return to keep house for her bullying father when her mother left him, she is quite often used to represent a view of a younger generation which is shiftless, selfish and unreliable. Alternately the girlfriend (indeed seducer) and tormentor of Steve Fisher, she left him behind in Weatherfield while she sought the bright lights of London. She returned (in the high-powered car of a middle-aged Lothario) a sadder but not wiser woman, and was eventually re-engaged by Steve to work for Baldwin again. She left for London in December 1979 intending to join Steve, who had been transferred to Baldwin's London factory.

Deirdre Langton (Anne Kirkbride), *née* Hunt, b.1955, m. Ray Langton 1975, divorced 1979, daughter Tracy 1977.
Deirdre worked as a secretary for the firm of Fairclough and Langton from 1973. She was engaged for a time to Billy Walker, but broke off the affair for very nebulous reasons in June 1975. Picked up by Ray Langton after a very stormy scene, she married him in July of that year. They eventually moved into 5 Coronation Street (the house that Mike Baldwin had had done up for Bet Lynch). Deirdre is customarily hot-tempered and resilient but was much altered first by a sexual assault, then by Ray's affair with a waitress in Dawson's Café in 1978, and lastly by the temporary loss of her daughter whom she feared dead. She is back on form currently, but still somewhat more vulnerable than she was, as in her affair with Ken Barlow when she was very hurt by his initial inclination to disown the connection with her when Ray threatened to cite him in his divorce proceedings. When she sold her own home she went to live with Emily Bishop at No. 3, and on the occasion of Emily's marriage to Arnold Swain she moved into the flat at the corner shop, where she now helps Alf Roberts since Renee's death.

MARRIAGEABLE MEN

(a) Mature, sexy men
Mike Baldwin (Johnny Briggs), b.1942.
Born in a basement flat in South London and educated at the local secondary modern school, Mike Baldwin has worked his way up in the world from tea-boy, via a television and radio repair business in the front bedroom, to factory owner. He entered Coronation Street in 1976 when he bought the then disused Warehouse and converted it into his second factory for making

trendy denim clothing under the name Baldwin's Casuals. He also owned a retail shop called The Western Front which he bought as an outlet for his clothes and which he closed in 1978. He employs, or has employed, many of the people in the street, including Suzie, Ernest Bishop, Steve Fisher, Hilda Ogden, Elsie Tanner, Gail Tilsley, Ivy Tilsley. He lives in a hotel in Weatherfield. His attempt to bring more comfort into his life by setting up Bet Lynch as housekeeper/mistress at No. 5 Coronation Street broke down when she found he was not, as he had claimed, already married and therefore unable to marry her. The Rovers Return is his usual centre (if only so that he may check up on his work force, who customarily gather there) and he was injured when a lorry crashed into The Rovers in 1979.

Len Fairclough (Peter Adamson), b.1924, m.(1) Nellie Briggs 1949, son Stanley 1950, divorced 1963 (died 1964); m.(2) Rita Littlewood 1977.
Len Fairclough was in the Royal Navy in the war, and then worked (after an abbreviated wartime brick-laying apprenticeship) for several building firms before setting up on his own in 1962. He has been self-employed ever since, sometimes in partnership (with Jerry Booth 1965–1968, and with Ray Langton 1970–1978) and sometimes on his own as he has been since Ray walked out. He is a local councillor. He has had several affairs, including a long-running one with Elsie Tanner, whom he has several times asked to marry him; one with Janet Reid (later Ken Barlow's wife) to whom he was engaged in 1969; one with Bet Lynch in 1975, which broke up when he refused to live with her; and most recently with Rita Littlewood, by whom he eventually did the decent thing.

(b) Fearful, withdrawn types
Ken Barlow (William Roache), b.1939, m.(1) Valerie Tatlock (Albert's niece) 1962, son Peter and daughter Susan 1963, Valerie died in 1971, electrocuted by a faulty hair-dryer plug; m.(2) Janet Reid 1973, no children, Janet committed suicide in 1977.
Ken Barlow lives with his first wife's uncle, Albert Tatlock, at No. 1 Coronation Street – a fitting address for two characters who have been present since the first episode of the serial. His father was a Post Office supervisor, and Ken is a scholarship boy who eventually took a degree in English and History at Manchester University. His mother died in an accident in 1961 and his father and brother are now also dead. His children live with Valerie's mother in Glasgow. Ken is presented as an eminently respectable do-gooder, despite having had a very unsettled career as, variously, personnel officer, teacher, writer, warehouse executive, taxi-driver. In 1969 he went to jail for supporting a banned anti-Vietnam war demonstration (the cause he was really supporting being that of free speech) and he has been seen involved in fist fights with Len Fairclough. He is currently Community Development Officer. He has had, again despite his eminent respectability, several affairs both between and during his marriage, and most recently

75

with Deirdre Langton.

Fred Gee (Fred Feast), b.1934, m. Edna Blanchard, who died in a fire at the Warehouse in 1975.

Fred has been resident bar/cellarman at The Rovers Return since 1976, and is occasionally called into service as Mrs Walker's chauffeur. He claims a sometimes lubricious interest in women but has not been seen to have any success in his – in any case faint-hearted – pursuit of: 1. Vera Duckworth, who returned to her husband; 2. a local barmaid, Alma Walsh, whom he hoped to gain as a wife largely because the local brewery had promised him a pub of his own if he were to marry; 3. Rita Littlewood, who preferred Len Fairclough.

Alf Roberts (Bryan Mosley), b.1926, m.(1) Phyllis Plant 1946, who died 1972; m.(2) Renee Bradshaw 1978, who died 1980.

Alf was formerly a Post Office supervisor until he joined his second wife Renee Bradshaw, in the corner shop after an accident which left him excessively tired and uncharacteristically rude and ill-tempered. Alf's shyness with women is often a source of humour in the programme (as when Bet once pretended to be trying to seduce him during Renee's absence from the shop and he was shown repeatedly in physical retreat from her). Similarly he is sometimes mocked by 'manly' men like Len Fairclough or Ray Langton. None the less he has had a series of affairs: even during his first marriage he had an affair with Maggie Clegg of the corner shop, and after his first wife's death he proposed to her; in 1975 he was conned by an attractive stranger who pretended to fancy him and whom he took into his home, eventually lending her £500 to set up a hairdressing business, at which she promptly disappeared; he conducted (or more exactly was led through) a protracted, pained courtship of Renee Bradshaw. With Renee's death he is again 'available', if only, so far, for the teasing of someone like Deirdre.

Albert Tatlock (Jack Howarth), b.1895, m.1919, daughter Beatrice 1923, widower 1959.

Born into a family of weavers, Albert was educated at a factory school and worked mornings from the age of 8. He served as an immediate volunteer in the Lancashire Fusiliers from 1914–1919, and won the Military Medal. He still despises those who did not fight, and hates the 'Jerries'. He was unemployed during the Depression, but in 1933 he became full-time steward of the local Labour Club. During World War II he became a local government clerk until his official retirement. He has contrived to work since then, first as lollipop man, then as assistant caretaker at the Community Centre. He has been, despite his age and suspicion of others, the centre of several marriage plots: in 1965 a widow proposed to him but they decided eventually that it would not work out; in 1969 he got as far as the altar with another widow but the vicar's late arrival gave him time to change his mind; in 1973 he proposed to Minnie Caldwell on the grounds that a joint household would be more economical than separate ones, but he again backed out, daunted by the thought of marital obligations. Albert is a notoriously stingy character, drinking his favourite rum only when someone else is paying, and otherwise sticking to mild. He has none of the mellowness of the older women in the programme, nor is he, as they customarily are, necessarily in the right. Only with his grandson is he sometimes shown to have more understanding than younger people.

(c) Conventional young men
Steve Fisher (Laurence Mullin), b.1957.
After leaving college in 1977 with qualifications as a technician, Steve took a stopgap job as van driver for Mike Baldwin. Eventually Baldwin offered him a job as trainee manager. Somewhat soft for life in Coronation Street, he is variously the victim of Ivy Tilsley's tongue, Mike Baldwin's bullying, or, notably, the importunities of Suzie Birchall, by whom he was seduced. He is often torn between a sense of general goodwill and fairness and his responsibilities to Mike Baldwin. In December 1979 he was transferred to the London factory to gain more experience, and Suzie followed him there.

Brian Tilsley (Christopher Quinten), b.1958, m. Gail Potter 1979, son 1980.
Brian entered *Coronation Street* in December 1978 as an apprentice motor mechanic studying for ONC at night-school and mad on motorbikes. He dated Gail from the first, eventually selling his motorbike because of her distaste for it. He married Gail at least partially against his mother's wishes, even though Ivy sought out information about Gail's earlier affair. They lived with his parents at No. 5 Coronation Street until they were able to buy a house in a new estate with the help of a (sacrificial) loan from Brian's parents. Their mortgage repayments were threatened by Brian's dismissal from work, but he was reinstated in time to celebrate the birth of his son.

MARRIED COUPLES

Hilda and Stan Ogden (Jean Alexander and Bernard Youens), Hilda *née* Crabtree b.1924, Stan b.1922, m.1943, daughter Freda (who calls herself Irma) 1946, son Trevor 1949, grandchildren 1972, 1976.
The Ogdens live, with heavy irony, at No. 13 Coronation Street. Stan has had various jobs since he ceased work as a lorry driver in 1964. He was a milkman from 1964–1965, then bought an ice-cream business which failed, worked as a night-watchman in 1969 until he was sacked for sleeping on the job, bought his present window-cleaning round in 1972 and has worked at this in a desultory way ever since. His attempts at self-employment are not made in pursuit of advancement, but rather as an avoidance of the hard work that employers might demand of him. He is notably obtuse, even when

he affects a low cunning in search of his only loves, beer and laziness. Hilda is a cleaner at The Rovers Return in the mornings, and has more recently worked as a cleaner at Baldwin's Casuals in the evenings too. She is only slightly less of a slut than Stan, but differs from him in having a certain urchin quickness. It is usually her thick skin rather than lack of ability that makes her slow to pick up insults. Their marriage is the most (the only) lasting one in Coronation Street, though even it has occasionally been threatened, as when Stan left home tired of being nagged, and was comforted by the helper in his brother-in-law's fish and chip shop.

Bert and Ivy Tilsley (Peter Dudley and Lynne Perrie), Bert b.1935, Ivy b.1936, son Brian 1958.

The Tilsleys live at No. 5 Coronation Street, which they bought from Deirdre Langton after the break-up of her marriage. Bert is a quiet, easy-going shift-worker at Fosters Iron Foundry. He is a conscientious and loyal member of his union. He allows Ivy to dominate him when he alone loses by it, but stands up to her firmly when she bullies others, as in her attempts to stop Brian seeing Gail. He is currently very depressed since he has been made redundant. Ivy is a much more fiery character, who has organised strike action at Baldwin's Casuals on two occasions. (It is well within the conventions of the programme that even strikes should be seen as the result of temperamental/psychological make-up.) Ivy disapproved of Brian's marriage to Gail, partly because Gail is not a Roman Catholic, but more on the grounds that she was losing her son. Now that Gail is part of the family she tends to be possessive about both of them, and lent them her and Bert's holiday savings towards the deposit for their new home.

ROGUES

(a) Ne'er-do-wells
Dennis Tanner, b.1942, m.1968, divorced.
When the programme started, Dennis Tanner had just been discharged from borstal after being found guilty of persistent shop-lifting. He worked intermittently as a bouncer in a local nightclub, set up a theatrical agency in his bedroom, or rented out theatrical digs when his mother was away. In 1967 he went to live in a hippy commune where he fell for Jenny Sutton. He moved to Bristol on his wedding night, after borrowing an unreturned £125 from Elsie. There was news in 1973 that he was in jail for swindling old-age pensioners with a double-glazing con trick.

Ray Langton (Neville Buswell), b.1947, m. Deirdre Hunt 1975, daughter 1977, divorced 1979.
As a boy, Ray served a sentence in borstal. By training (received in reform school) he is a plumber and joiner. He worked for Len Fairclough but was sacked for stealing. He was jailed for two years for breaking and entering. In

1968 he was taken back by Fairclough, and in 1970 became a junior partner in the business and lived with Fairclough. In 1975 he married Deirdre Hunt after a whirlwind courtship, and in 1977 they moved into No. 5 when their daughter Tracy was born. Ray appeared to be a reformed character, but in 1978 he had an affair with an attractive young waitress at Dawson's Café. The marriage broke down and he went to work in Holland where Deirdre refused to join him. In 1979 he told Deirdre that he wanted a divorce.

Billy Walker (Kenneth Farrington), b.1938.
Annie Walker's cherished son has been offered (and refused) every advantage: he was expelled from his private school for fighting; he has consistently failed to make use of his training as a motor mechanic; he betrayed his trust as manager for his mother at The Rovers Return and had to leave after stealing £200. He has twice been the owner of a local garage in Weatherfield. In 1975 he became manager of a hotel in Jersey, and in 1979 touched his mother for £2,000 to buy a partnership in a bar in Jersey. He has four times been on the brink of marriage, but on each occasion the affair has broken down, on three of them with a little help from his mother. In some ways he might fit better in the group of mature, attractive men (as, indeed, Mike Baldwin might fit better here) but his persistent appearances on the fringe of the law (arrested on suspicion of stealing suede jackets, for example, in 1974) and his treatment of vulnerable characters like Bet puts him more centrally in the category of rogue.

Eddie Yeats (Geoffrey Hughes), b.1941.
A native of Liverpool, Eddie Yeats first appeared at Minnie Caldwell's in 1974 on Christmas parole from prison in place of another of Minnie's protégés, Jed Stone. In spite of Ena Sharples' advice, Minnie invited him to stay. He has been in trouble from boyhood, and finished his education in borstal. He has so far spent a total of seven years in prison. He has been involved in two incidents with the law since 1974, first stacking the loot for friends after a supermarket robbery (which finished with his return to jail since he had in any case overstayed his parole) and then getting a six-month sentence for supplying to his burglar friends information which he got while on the window-cleaning round with Stan Ogden. Eddie was no more industrious than Stan Ogden as a partner on the round, and Hilda intervened to get rid of him by declaring herself company director and then sacking him. Despite his reluctance to work and his light fingers, Eddie often displays a flamboyant sensitivity and a practical resourcefulness. He was, for example, the one who saved Bet Lynch from suicide, the only one able to make Ken's Community Centre attractive to small children (and decent enough to stand down without a fuss when parents objected to having their children in the care of an ex-con), and the one who provided real companionship for Minnie Caldwell.

(b) Confidence tricksters

There have been many confidence tricksters, but it is difficult to give details here since they are almost always, and by definition, outsiders who appear only at the moment of the playing of the trick. Residence outside Weatherfield and/or a fluent deployment of Standard English speech are the symbols of deceit. Billy Walker, now living (significantly) in the south, is one rather specialised, recurrent example; Mike Baldwin, though always well within the law, is another. Of the incidental appearances one might cite the following as typical: 1969 – the men who disappeared after taking £20 from Minnie Caldwell for the pointing of her house; 1975 – the shower salesmen who took £20 'advance payment' from Ena Sharples (and were eventually brought to book by Eddie and Len); 1975 – Annie Walker's cousin, Charles Beaumont, who pretended to be staying at the 'Midland' and borrowed money from Annie's friends and clients; 1975 – Post Office worker Donna Parker who wormed her way into the affections of a bemused Alf Roberts, borrowed £500 to set up a hairdressing business, and disappeared; 1980 – pet-shop owner Arnold Swain, who tried to get Emily to invest money and eventually married her bigamously.

RICHARD PATERSON AND JOHN STEWART

Street Life

The other essays in this collection deal with particular aspects of *Coronation Street*, and in this essay we want to map out the textual operation of two specific episodes – numbers 1822 and 1823 – which were transmitted on 3 and 5 July 1978. They are two of six episodes which are available for hire on videocassette from the BFI Film and Video Library.*

Christine Geraghty has considered the formal characteristics of continuous serial narrative elsewhere in this publication. The interweaving of separate stories over a number of episodes and the continual postponement of a final resolution, or lack of closure, make the formal analysis of the narrative of a single episode problematic. As Geraghty states, 'much of the work which has been done on narrative has concentrated on works which are read with the knowledge that they will come to an end'. What characterises *Coronation Street*, however, is continuity: individual stories *may* be resolved (often only temporarily) but the serial must carry on.

Before proceeding to examine the textual operation of the individual episodes, it would seem useful to place them and the individual stories contained in them within the context of the narrative continuity of the serial. It is obviously impossible to provide a total context which embraces the 2,000 plus episodes of *Coronation Street* (though a brief account of the major story lines was given in the *TV Times* Souvenir album 'Coronation Street 2,000'), but what can be given is a detailed description of the organisation of narrative strands running through the episodes bordering on the two under scrutiny. For this purpose we shall examine the preceding four episodes, 1818 to 1821, and the ensuing four episodes, 1824 to 1827, thus offering a picture of the narrative development of the serial over ten episodes.

The more detailed examination of episodes 1822 and 1823 is based upon reading the camera scripts and viewing cassettes of those episodes, but the description of the narrative progression of episodes 1818 to 1821 and 1824 to 1827 is based upon only the story outlines for those episodes. Each one carries the warning: 'These story outlines are only an indication of what will appear on screen. They may be subject to dramatic changes.' And indeed the script of episode 1823 differs significantly from the story outline. Similarly the actual episode as transmitted may differ slightly from the camera script.

In the story outlines produced by the *Coronation Street* production office, these plots, stories or narrative strands are referred to as 'themes', and the

* 127 Charing Cross Road, London WC2H 0EA.

81

usual practice is to have a 'main theme' and one or more 'secondary themes', as indicated in the following examples.

Episode 1818
Main Theme: Mike stands fast on his decision to fire Hilda – and the factory girls come out on strike.
Secondary Theme: Alf gets embarrassed when people catch on to Bet's 'togetherness' tactics with him. Elsie returns – and announces she's reverting from Mrs Howard to Mrs Tanner.

Episode 1819
Main Theme: Mike and Steve's plan to drive through the picket line is foiled by the strikers.
Secondary Theme: Alf realises that gossip about himself and Bet alone in the shop is rife and he goes back to stay in his old house.

The practice of paralleling a serious theme – the strike – with a comic one – the gossip about Alf and Bet – is evident from this example.

Over the five-week period covering the ten episodes under consideration the following seven narrative strands are interwoven:

1. The strike at Baldwin's factory following Hilda Ogden's dismissal (this itself has a 'comic' subsidiary narrative strand of Hilda obtaining another job).
2. The gossip surrounding the relationship between Alf Roberts and his lodger Bet Lynch while his wife Renee is away. Bet's attempt to move elsewhere on Renee's return.
3. The return of Elsie Tanner to the street and her old job at Baldwin's.
4. Fred Gee's brief courtship of Alma Walsh to get a pub of his own.
5. The purchase of a new bed for Ena Sharples with money collected from 'regulars' by Eddie Yeats and Emily Bishop.
6. The taking in and protection of a battered wife, Brenda Ditchburn, by Emily Bishop.
7. Antagonism between Ray Langton and Len Fairclough resulting from the collapse of an important building contract.

The progression of these narrative strands and their combination in each episode can be represented diagramatically (see Fig.3).

This diagram is of course extremely schematic, though it does offer a picture of the placing of the narrative strands over ten episodes. It is evident from the diagram that narrative strands are not necessarily continuous in the sense of their being present in each episode; they can 'drop out' for two or three episodes before being resumed (e.g., Elsie Tanner's return and the Alf/Bet/Renee relationship). The diagram does not effectively show the relative weighting of each narrative strand in terms of time devoted to them. As Geraghty notes, 'It is a characteristic of the continuous serial that two or

Fig. 3

Episode 'Theme'	1818	1819	1820	1821	1822	1823	1824	1825	1826	1827
The Strike	M.T.	M.T.	S.T.	P.	M.T.	M.T.				
Alf/Bet/Renee	S.T.	S.T.	M.T.	S.T.			S.T.	M.T.		
Elsie's return	S.T.	P.				P.	P.	P.		
Fred and Alma			P.	M.T.	P.	P.				
Ena's bed					S.T.	S.T.	M.T.	M.T.		
Emily and Brenda								P.	M.T.	M.T.
Ray vs. Len									S.T.	S.T.

M.T. = Main Theme
S.T. = Secondary Theme
as indicated in story outlines
P. = Presence of theme in subsidiary way.

three stories being dealt with are given approximately equal time in each episode', and this is broadly true of the main and secondary themes indicated. Other narrative strands present but in a subsidiary way are of course devoted less time – for example, Fred and Alma's courtship is present in only one scene in episode 1822. It should be noted that even after a particular narrative strand has reached some sort of 'temporary resolution' and therefore appears closed, it can reappear (often in conversation) as a 'memory trace' of past events. Episode 1826 contains references to the strike at Baldwin's directly and Fred and Alma's courtship obliquely; though neither of these is indicated on the diagram. In a similar way, prior to their main development, narrative strands may be prefigured or 'set up' by clues and references – for example, the importance of the Langton-Fairclough hotel building contract and the possibility of conflict between Ray and Len is signalled in episode 1822. This episode also contains hints at difficulties in the relationship between Ray Langton and his wife Deirdre which prefigures Ray's subsequent extra-marital affair with Janice Stubbs some ten weeks later in episodes 1845 and 1846.

As Geraghty points out, the existing approaches to narrative analysis assume discrete texts. Their application to the continuous serial is very problematic, being unable to take account of the overarching reference points or the episodic form of the serial narrative. (Cf. Roger Silverstone for an outline of the various theories of narrative, in *The Message of Television*.) Our method of analysis examines the oppositions operative in the serial. This approach, which owes much to Lévi-Strauss, seeks to uncover the concealed structures of the text within its cultural framework. That is, it is our purpose here to interrupt the smooth surface of the text in these two episodes to examine how oppositions construct the narrative within the serial's referential field.

It is possible to see the major oppositions of *Coronation Street* as Inside:Outside and Male:Female. However, in these episodes an additional opposition, Work:No-Work, dominates the narrative; employment questions act as the hinge of the narrative, allowing an integration of the many narrative strands particular to these episodes within the continuing mythic reality. These are traced through various forms of interplay between characters within the major themes of the episodes – the strike at the factory over Hilda's dismissal, and the discovery that Ena Sharples' bad back is caused by her old bed. At the same time the various stylistic elements – the narrative space and the visual appurtenances – contribute signs of continuity in the mythic reality of *Street* life and are the foundations upon which the specific narrative elements are constructed.

Episode 1822 opens in the Kabin – along with the Rovers Return one of the most important centres of gossip exchange, communal sites crucial to the intersection and interweaving of the various narrative strands.

EDDIE *(to Mavis)*: Afternoon, love, afternoon. It's just gone twelve *(Picking up a morning newspaper from counter top*). So you'll not get rid of this paper now, will you? Nobody's going to buy a morning paper when it's afternoon.

Most viewers bring to each episode they watch a certain familiarity with the *Street* and its characters. Such knowledge is assumed to the extent that openings expect *viewer* knowledge and episode 1822 is no exception. Eddie is immediately marked as scrounging. He functions as an index of the episode's main concern – constantly referred to through the play of oppositions – that of work. This is further marked when Eddie continues:

EDDIE: Eh? Ah yes, but I'm different from the common herd, aren't I? I mean, being a gentleman of leisure I've only rolled out of me pit, so to me this is still like early morning.

The opposition between those in work and those out of work is immediately established – the notion of unemployment is brought into play and integrated as a part of our *Street* knowledge. The scene also reintroduces the strikers (an existing theme), who are sitting in the café section *and* introduces the narrative strand about Ena's illness. Thus the major and secondary themes are interwoven in this place of exchange – marking the major oppositions at play in this episode through established characters and with references to the audience's *Street* memory.

The differentiation of 'striking' and 'scrounging' as no-work elements is incorporated in an exchange between Ivy and Eddie (Fig.4) which also sets out a key opposition in the mythic history of the *Street* – Men:Women (cf. Jordan).

EDDIE: I don't know what's happened to women these days. They don't want to give a bloke hard work and good service any more. I mean, look at you lot.
VERA (*a little later*): It's all right for layabouts like you, you're drawing all sorts, social security, dole, everything. We're drawing nowt.

Work:No-Work is an opposition integrated into the narrative of this episode in different ways, and it is difficult confidently to identify a particular set of attitudes and values as dominant. Because *Coronation Street* is a continuous serial with a past, the posing of a simple enigma is not possible. The invocation of scroungers and state welfare is mapped across the opposition Male:Female, using our knowledge of the street characters involved. The following scene adds another element to the opposition Work:No-Work as Mike Baldwin (at the factory) tells Steve, his assistant, that he has decided to use blackleg labour to keep the company in business. Mike Baldwin – the factory owner – is an insider of sorts, but still suspect because of his London background, and marked by his exploitation of women (he employs them; he also considers himself a lady's man).

MIKE: I don't care what you call them; as far as I'm concerned they're willing to work. And that's all I'm interested in.

Implicit in this confrontational attitude – a test of the strikers' resolve – is the gender opposition mapped on class oppositions. However, what is most significantly introduced by this decision is the Inside:Outside opposition. The mythic reality of the Street community is threatened by outsiders willing to do the work of insiders. The ever present necessity of Street life to expel intruders marks this as a double threat, and a site of disruption.

Within the fictional space of *Coronation Street,* characters often step directly from the Street into other characters' living rooms, there being no lobby or hallway. 'Every front door hides a story. Seven front doors, twenty interesting people' was how the earliest episodes were described in *TV Times.* The sense of community of the insiders is strongly signified not only by interchanges in communal spaces – The Kabin, The Rovers – but also by this proximity and the social practice of 'popping in' to see people. On the rare occasions when characters refuse visitors and shut themselves away in private it is usually at a time of crisis and a dramatic disruption of the equilibrium of community: for example, Bet Lynch, after the news of her illegitimate son's death; Emily Swain/Bishop after the discovery that she had contracted a bigamous marriage.

The street as a community concerned with its own is invoked when Emily, after her earlier enquiries at the Kabin about why Ena had been to hospital had drawn a blank, goes to Ena's house (Fig.5).

EMILY: Hello Mrs Sharples. I just thought I'd pop round and say hello.

Our knowledge of the Emily Bishop character is used here – her current paramedical role at the hospital and the memory of her husband Ernest's recent death. Beyond this is an additional knowledge of her 'uprightness'; differentiating her from the Elsie Tanner-type characters.

EMILY: I didn't mean to offend you. I just know it's easy to neglect yourself when you're on your own. I've found that out these last few months.

This scene takes place in Ena's front room, which is marked by its visual appurtenances. Memory of the mythic reality of Ena's character-text (with the hair-net the most distinctive feature) is placed within a set which has a distinctive significational input – old photographs, a Welsh dresser with blue and white crockery, etc. Narrative drive is constantly underpinned by the visual signification in each scene (Fig.6). The Work:No-Work opposition is again invoked in their conversation.

ENA: They keep you on the go at that place by the look of it.

Fig. 4   *Fig. 5*

Fig. 6   *Fig. 7*

Fig. 8   *Fig. 9*

And the scene's coda maintains the persistent integration of this opposition through repetition.

ENA: How serious can anything be at my time of life? Can't keep me off work, can it, because I haven't got any work . . . If you must know it's a bit of back trouble.

Here there is a counterpointing of narrative themes – the main one, of employment, is further integrated, while the secondary thematic is recast. The initial enigma – what is wrong with Ena? – is partially solved. This allows a redirection of the narrative strand towards finding a solution and enables the drawing in of community support (i.e. self-help rather than state help is the preferred solution – Inside:Outside).

The next scene is the first in the bar of the Rovers Return. The Rovers is the space in the *Street* where all narrative strands are brought together, frequently with a dexterity of camera use not seen in other sets. We 'know' the place – it is always there, always the same. Just as the long-standing characters carry complicated meanings, so the space underpins a narrative based on memory – not just of character and event, but also of visual signification and style.

The scene opens in the Rovers with Fred and Annie discussing the strike, with Mike Baldwin, the troubled employer, seen in the background going through his papers (Fig.7).

FRED: Bit on the quiet side this dinner, Mrs Walker.
ANNIE: Yes, I blame those women across the street.

Annie acts as the 'aristocrat' of the street; but there is no general acceptance of these 'airs', which are continually undermined by other *Street* characters. An outline of the 'problem' for business people caused by strikes is followed by an employer's perspective on work.

ANNIE: A licensee has many, many headaches, Fred. The responsibility is a heavy burden.

At this point Annie the employer literally replaces Mike the employer in the frame. The division between employer and employee (again operating around the cardinal function of employment) is focused by Annie's interest in her employees' welfare, which is in fact just as much self-interest because of the brewery's insistence that a man be resident on the premises. Her enquiries about Fred's romantic involvements also gently invoke gender opposition: Fred didn't propose because Alma was too bossy – in fact like Annie.

The mobility of the camera is used to reintroduce Mike Baldwin, who had been 'lost' off-camera (Fig.8); the camera pans round as he orders a drink.

Steve's arrival allows the problems of employers to be further explained, since he has had no success in finding women to work that night, so:

MIKE: Usual thing. If you want a job doing, you've got to do it yourself . . .

The camera then pans with Mike as he leaves the bar and stops with Len and Elsie as they are joined by Deirdre (Fig.9). The interweaving of the narrative is maintained by one camera as it moves round the Rovers bar. The work and gender oppositions mapped over one another dominate the ensuing dialogue. The characters involved – Len, Elsie, Deirdre – allow the viewer to bring to the scene a wealth of knowledge, so that when Deirdre says 'he' there is no need for explanation that she is talking of Ray, or that Elsie's disillusionment with men comes from bitter experience, or that Len is Ray's partner.

DEIRDRE: (*of Ray*) He's working through his dinner time these days. This hotel job, you know. He's really putting the hours in.

The duplicity of the text at this point is significant – Ray's thoughtlessness prefigures his infidelity in future episodes (see above). Elsie's understanding of Deirdre's problems with her husband is based on her history – our memory of her often unhappy relationships with men.

DEIRDRE: Out of bed this morning, why isn't my breakfast on the table, where's my clean underpants, this fried egg's hard, give us my butties, tara.

ELSIE: That's men, love. They're all the same, even Ray.

This scene also allows a marking out of women's work as part of the key opposition of Men:Women. In other words, women's work is seen as not being part of the world of 'real' work which men occupy.
   Meanwhile Emily has appeared in frame in deep focus at the bar, obviously looking for someone (Fig.10). The frame is used to introduce characters to the space of the narrative. There is then a cut to Emily and Albert in the snug (Fig.11). The snug was in earlier episodes colonised by Ena, Minnie and Martha, and is still used most often by older street characters. Emily enquires of Albert about Ena's back trouble – marking here the concern for old people but resolved in gender opposition, as Albert shows no concern and on being sternly rebuked by Emily exclaims in exasperation, 'Women'. Albert's cantankerousness and self-reliance require little signalling as we are assumed to be familiar with his character and views.
   The action then shifts to the Ogdens' living room and, as is usually the case with the Ogdens, is marked by humour. The room itself signifies in a number of ways the 'difference' of the Ogdens: the mural with added flying ducks in particular (Fig.12); Hilda's curlers and mac; Stan's appetite and

love of beer; even the shape of the characters – Stan's corpulence, Hilda's leanness – are continual reminders that the Ogdens are joke characters.

A comic sub-theme operates within the theme of the strike. The strike was called over Hilda's dismissal from Baldwin's, provoked by her demands for a new brush (she was employed as a cleaner), but Stan has found Hilda a new job. Hilda's treachery in keeping secret her new job from the strikers demanding her reinstatement would seem to belie the Inside:Outside opposition. The Ogdens' status as insiders, accepted members of the community, is complicated, however, by their 'difference', much humour resting on their attempts to be accepted or revered/envied by the street. The scene opens with Stan seated eating a kipper.

STAN: I like kippers – they give you a thirst.

Hilda is about to leave for her new job at the abattoir. This work potentially undermines her 'woman's' work, looking after Stan, which is a double responsibility marking gender opposition.

STAN: I'm entitled to have my tea ready for me after a hard day's work.
HILDA: Hard day's work. You don't know what it is. And any road, it were you got me this evening cleaning job, so don't start moaning. It's self, self, self with you, first, last and in the middle.

When Ivy arrives to enlist Hilda for picket duty, Hilda's attempted excuse of going to bingo is refused. The incursion of outsiders into the Ogden household causes their internal divisions to heal rapidly as they face the world – their 'difference' from the rest of the world creates a unity when confronted by it.

Part One ends with a poser: Mike sets Steve the task of preparing the machines ready for the night shift. Another test for the strikers is signalled: will they successfully overcome this latest threat as they have the previous two (attempts to sub-contract work)? (Fig.13)

Part Two opens in the Rovers bar. Annie invites Emily to join her in a glass of sherry – two ladies of quality – but is spurned because Emily wishes to talk to Eddie about Ena (Fig.14). The site of their exchange – at one of the tables away from the bar (a confidential space often used for non-public interchange) – allows the 'story' to remain private. Emily seeks Eddie's help in discovering the cause of Ena's back trouble. Eddie, as social Samaritan 'working' to maintain the welfare of the community, is marked against his lack of employment and his past. In doing this, Eddie's history of geniality, helping others and his great concern for the old is used – for example, his lodging with Minnie. The inside of the community here overrides other oppositions, e.g. Work: No-Work. Rebuffed, Annie's comments to Emily after Eddie has left have a significance which draws on the history of the *Street* and Eddie and Annie's characters.

Fig. 10

Fig. 11

Fig. 12

Fig. 13

Fig. 14

Fig. 15

ANNIE: If you're having any difficulty with that one, dear, any unpleasantness at all, just let me know.

Thus a contradictory assessment of Eddie is being offered (and implicitly of Annie also). Eddie was recently barred from the Rovers and the occasion when Eddie got her a monogrammed carpet (from a bingo hall) is recalled by Annie. Eddie's 'deals' and Annie's vanity, part of a viewer's knowledge, allow a humorous juxtaposition.

The following scene in the Kabin again marks women's work and gender opposition, centred round Deirdre's problems with Ray. The Mavis character enables a differentiation of women within work and life situations – Mavis the shop assistant and the perpetual spinster adores children, which motivates Deirdre's reply.

DEIRDRE: You don't know the half of it, all the cleaning and feeding, and seeing to. And the worry, starting with whether there's anything wrong with her, to whether something's going to happen to her . . .

Despite her problems of motherhood and a forgetful husband she is 'lucky'. The difference Men:Women is further marked by Albert's self-reliant cantankerousness asserting itself again as he first outpaces Elsie to the door, and then complains and gets his money back on some sweets (Fig.15).

ELSIE: . . . Like I was saying in the Rovers this dinner, men are a pain in the neck. All ego like him, or dead casual like your Ray, forgetting your anniversary, all take and no give.

Finally the memory of Elsie's many unhappy relationships is directly invoked.

DEIRDRE: . . . I think you've just been a bit unlucky with your fellers.

The episode then proceeds to unravel further the enigmas around Ena's back trouble. Eddie, having 'popped in' to see Ena and scrounge his tea, enquires about the cause of the back trouble. He has gone to the house (at Emily's request) to act on behalf of the community. The problem is explained – a further progression of the narrative becomes possible. We are told that it is the bed that is the main problem: it is old and worn out, discussion of which allows some nostalgia – 'they made things better in them days' – but also a gentle reinvocation and repetition of the opposition Work:No Work.

EDDIE: . . . You need it. And anyway, you spend a lot of time in bed.
ENA: Not as much as most, I'll be bound. You included.

92

The rest of the episode rapidly advances the theme of the strike, again interweaving major oppositions in complicated overlapping of elements. As Hilda deserts Muriel on the picket line, the blackleg labour arrives. It is interesting that these women are marked as outsiders not only to the street (though two of them were former Baldwin employees before they were dismissed), but also to the region. The chief spokeswoman has a distinct Geordie accent. Muriel reports excitedly to the Rovers Return – disruption of the community by the incursion of outsiders directly touches the community's centre. Annie loses control temporarily – 'I won't have this shouting in my pub.' Then as there is general pandemonium outside the factory (minibus tyres let down; a beer glass thrown through a window; shouting), there is a shot of Annie and Len outside the Rovers (Fig.16).

ANNIE: I can't believe it's happening. Not in *this* street.
LEN: Wherever it happens – it's always somebody's street.

The episode ends with disruption of the street mapped against the serial mythology of a community able to solve its own problems, while referring out to a media mythology of strikes. The final shot pulls back from the factory gates as the women demonstrate, and the resolution of this narrative strand is left for the Wednesday episode.

Wednesday's episode (1823) opens with a continuation of the final shots from episode 1822 (Fig.17). There is no elapsed time between episodes – a device which is used, as Geraghty points out, only in exceptional circumstances of narrative tension. The comments from the chorus at the Rovers continue, led by Annie's laments.

ANNIE: People you thought you knew and suddenly they start behaving like . . . well, animals I suppose.

Inside the factory the women have discovered they are strike-breaking, not doing leisure shift-work. They refuse to use the machines, but are conned by Mike into staying inside. Women's solidarity is marked, as well as the duplicitous 'strategy' of employers (Mike wants the strikers to believe the women inside are working). With a continuing demonstration in the street, Annie takes the initiative in solving the problem by phoning for the police – outsiders, but agents of order. Annie is representing the street when she seeks to restore equilibrium, but in doing so crosses over the inside:outside opposition. The ideological work of the episode around the police counterpoints and attempts to rescue this contradiction. The women understand what Mike is up to and demand to leave. Just as Mike goes to call the police, a siren is heard responding to Annie's call. Once the police sergeant is inside the factory the exchange with Mike Baldwin refers to an assumed knowledge of the 'real world' (the bitter strike at the Grunwick factory in London, etc.).

SERGEANT: . . . Why didn't you let us know there might be trouble?

MIKE: I didn't know they were going to carry on like a bunch of werewolves, did I?

SERGEANT: (*Not very tolerant. He's seen it all before and isn't too impressed with Mike's air of innocence*) Oh, come on. You drive a bus load of strike-breakers into your factory and you didn't expect any trouble? (Fig.18).

In the Rovers the conversation reflects on the position of police in society.

FRED: Aye . . . like a red rag to bull is a copper's uniform to a lot of them. They reckon they're poking their noses in where they don't belong.

ANNIE: I remember when a police officer's uniform was something to command respect. What on earth this world's coming to I don't know.

Meanwhile Eddie's arrival at the Rovers allows a reintroduction of the Ena storyline, but only after a complicated dialogue around the interweaving oppositions Work:No-Work, Inside:Outside, and references to the real world and various contradictory positions on strikes, unemployment etc.

EDDIE: . . . Course. I blame the Government myself.

ELSIE: You want to watch it. They just might stop keeping you.

EDDIE (*a little later*): Stands to reason, doesn't it? If there wasn't so much unemployment, these lads I'm talking about wouldn't have time on their hands to go round the strikes.

ELSIE: And if there weren't so many strikes there wouldn't be so much unemployment.

FRED: Which your mates are helping to bring about . . .

Here, although Eddie's position is shown as unworked out (he is 'puzzled'), almost immediately he is shown to possess true knowledge about Ena's back trouble. He tells Emily that he has discovered that the bed is the cause. Emily offers to approach the Social Security (outsiders – the state) to see if she can be given one.

In the following scene, the women are escorted from the factory by the police and then we cut to Mike and Steve in the sewing room, with Mike proclaiming victory despite Steve's feelings of defeat (Fig.19).

The second part of the episode opens in the Ogdens' living room the next morning. Stan is eating liver that Hilda has brought home from her new job. Their conversation again marks the oppositions Men:Women and Work:No-Work – and their divided unity.

STAN: Best day's work I did when I got you that job.

HILDA: *You* might have got it, but it's me who has to go and do t'work, and don't you forget it.

STAN: (*chuckles*) All that lot carrying on last night 'cos you lost your job and you're the only one who's working.

Fig. 16

Fig. 17

Fig. 18

Fig. 19

Fig. 20

Fig. 21

This is placed within our knowledge of the Ogdens' marginal position in street life – the repetition of the element of humour also undercuts the motivation of the strike effort.

HILDA: Eh, it's a smashing feeling, though.
STAN: What is?
HILDA: Us Ogdens coming out on top for once in us lives.

Comment from the Rovers continues as Annie gives Fred orders, just as she is leaving for an appointment.

ANNIE: And remember. One inkling of any trouble from over the road, and you must phone the police immediately. I'm not standing for another second of it. This is a street of homes, not a battlefield!

The action shifts to Baldwin's factory for the meeting between Mike and Ivy which opens with Mike disconsolately holding the brush that was at the centre of the initial trouble as all the women enter the sewing room. The episode then moves to Emily's second visit to Ena. After Ena's comments on the strife in the street, Emily suggests an approach to the Social Security to obtain a new bed. Ena firmly refuses to countenance charity, i.e. outside help (Inside:Outside).

ENA: Look . . . I might not have much, but what I have got I've worked for and paid for, I've not taken a penny in charity since the day I was born.

An older value system and the notion of self-help predominate. There is also now a redirection of the narrative towards a resolution through community help.

The continual interweaving of the scenes of action (all closely related in fictional time) continues with the negotiations between Mike and Ivy, which result in an offer of reinstatement for Hilda. This is followed by Emily's initiation of a community collection in the Kabin for Mrs Sharples' new bed. Consideration at the factory gate of Mike Baldwin's offer is marked in a very strange way which can only be seen as reflecting dominant media representations of the time. The women are shown as a rabble, and Muriel, the one who wants to stay out (though she seconds the vote to return to work), makes her vote with a Nazi salute (Fig.20). Graffiti on the factory wall depict the Swastika and the Hammer and Sickle – images of extremism. All is recuperated in Mike Baldwin's comments on hearing of their return to work.

MIKE: . . . But just remember one thing. There aren't any winners in a situation like this. Only losers. Lost production, lost orders, lost profits, lost pay, lost goodwill. And where are we now? Back exactly where we were before it started.

96

That Steve has said as much at the outset is mentioned, but the statement comes across strongly as a straight political comment on 'strikes' in the real world, a familiar refrain on how industrial strife and class antagonism is damaging to the health of the community, the national interest. Resolution of this narrative strand also introduces the possibility of Elsie's return to her old job as supervisor, while having a comic finale in the necessity for the Ogdens to give up their new-found success, with Hilda *having* to return to the factory – 'or else!', as Vera says.

The episode ends in the Rovers – the community's central place where all can be brought back together and equilibrium restored. New narrative threads are tentatively established or redirected. So, Eddie's collection for Ena's bed reverberates initially with the oppositions of the rest of the narrative (Fig.21).

LEN: It's people like her who should be getting help, not flippin' spongers.

The scene then turns to humorous togetherness when Eddie ingratiates himself with Annie Walker, while putting the case for community help.

EDDIE: It's not for me. It's for Mrs Sharples. She's having this terrible back trouble, see, and she needs this new bed, but she can't afford it, can she? She won't ask for help from Social Security, so it's up to her mates to rally round.
ANNIE: For Mrs Sharples!
EDDIE: Right. That's why I thought you wouldn't mind me having a whip-round in here. If ever there was somebody who understands the meaning of pride, I thought, it's Mrs W. Sorry, Mrs Walker. She's the one person who would understand how Mrs Sharples feels. Go barefoot through the streets before she'd ask for a penny.

Elsie's reintegration into the street narrative (she had returned to the *Street* in episode 1818) – Mike offers her a job, and the viewer's memory is invoked when she says she wants to re-establish herself as the woman we used to know – sets up a poser for future episodes, encouragement for continued viewing.

What this analysis of two episodes brings out in particular is the variety of positions constructed for the viewer. No one set of attitudes and values is privileged in terms of dialogue, but a range of often contradictory positions is offered by the different characters working through the major oppositions. Thus the themes of *Coronation Street* episodes are worked out through the intertwining oppositions indicated, by characters with individually accumulating histories and a place in the overall mythology of *Street* life – a mythology which equally draws on the consistent use of sets. Pleasures in the text come not simply from the solving of enigmas through various snares but from deploying an ever-increasing knowledge of this mythic reality. Such a large lexical mythology exists prior to the introduction of narrative strands, so that the text can operate on many different levels according to the knowledge of the viewer. While it has proved possible to delineate the oppositions at work in these narrative strands and to indicate certain references out to the serial's past and to the real world, the possibility of differential appropriation by different members of the audience makes it, as Lovell indicates, an interesting and sometimes progressive site of cultural accumulation.

This plurality of 'ideologies' is dependent in large part on the serial's history. Its origin was as a community tale, but it relates to changes in British society in contradictory ways. After twenty years refracting social change through a basic set of characters represented as living in a 'working-class' community in northern England, its initial pluralism has multiplied and intensified, concretising a mythic reality that at times reverberates with the divisions of British society. This accumulation is still underpinned, however, by the nostalgic notion of 'community' that was dominant in representations of British working-class life in the late 1950s.

References

Althusser, L., *Essays in Self-Criticism,* New Left Books, London 1976.

Althusser, L., *Lenin and Philosophy and Other Essays,* New Left Books, London 1977.

Alvarado, M. and Buscombe, E., *Hazell: the Making of a TV Series,* BFI/Latimer, London 1978.

Annan, Lord (Chairman), *Report of the Committee on the Future of Broadcasting,* Cmnd. 6753, London 1977.

Barthes, R., *Système de la mode,* Paris 1967 (quoted in Culler).

Barthes, R., *S/Z* (trans. by R. Miller), Jonathan Cape, London 1975.

Black, P., *The Mirror in the Corner,* Hutchinson, London 1972.

Chanan, M., *Labour Power in the British Film Industry,* BFI, London 1976.

Chatman, S., *History and Discourse,* Cornell UP, Cornell 1978.

Comolli, J-L. and Narboni, J., 'Cinema/Ideology/Criticism', *Screen,* Vol. 12, No. 1, 1971.

Cook, J. and Lewington, M., *Images of Alcoholism,* BFI, London 1979.

Critcher, C., 'Sociology, Cultural Studies and the Post-War Working Class', in Clarke, J., et al. (*eds.*), *Working-Class Culture,* Hutchinson Educational, London 1979.

Culler, J., *Structuralist Poetics,* Routledge and Kegan Paul, London 1975.

Davies, G., 'Teaching About Narrative', *Screen Education,* No. 29, Winter 1978–9.

Dennis, N., et al., *Coal is Our Life: Analysis of a Yorkshire Mining Community,* Tavistock, London 1969.

Drummond, P., 'Structural and Narrative Constraints in "The Sweeney" ' in *Screen Education,* No. 20, Autumn 1976.

Dyer, R., 'Entertainment and Utopia', *Movie,* No. 22, 1976.

Dyer, R. (*ed.*), *Gays and Film,* BFI, London 1977.

Edmondson, M., and Rounds, D., *The Soaps: Daytime Serials of Radio and TV,* Stein and Day, New York 1973.

Fuller, P., *Seeing Berger,* Writers and Readers, London 1980.

Goldie, G.W., *Facing the Nation: Television and Politics 1936–1976,* Bodley Head, London 1977.

Goldthorpe, J., et al., *The Affluent Worker* (3 vols.), CUP, Cambridge 1968, 1969, 1969.

Goodhardt, G.J., Ehrenburg, A.S.C. and Collins, M.A., *The Television Audience: Patterns of Viewing,* Saxon House, Farnborough 1975.

Grabo, C., *Technique of the Novel,* New York 1928 (quoted in Chatman).

Gramsci, A., *Selections from Prison Notebooks* (trans. by Quintin Hoare and Geoffrey Nowell-Smith), Lawrence and Wishart, London 1971.

Hall, S., 'The Hinterland of Science: Ideology and the "Sociology of Knowledge" ', *Cultural Studies,* No. 10, 1977.

Harvey, S., *May '68 and Film Culture,* BFI, London 1978.

Heath, S. and Skirrow, G., 'Television – a World in Action', *Screen,* Vol. 18, No. 2, 1977.

Hoggart, R., *The Uses of Literacy,* Penguin, Harmondsworth 1969 (orig. 1957).

Hush, S. (see Thornber).

Jictar, *Weekly TV Audience Report,* Audits of Great Britain, Ruislip 1975, 1978, 1980.

Kershaw, H.V., *Coronation Street: Early Days,* Mayflower, St. Albans 1976.

Kershaw, H.V., *Trouble at the Rovers,* Mayflower, St. Albans 1976

Kershaw, H.V., *Elsie Tanner Fights Back,* Mayflower, St. Albans 1977.

Langer, S., *Feeling and Form,* Routledge and Kegan Paul, London 1953.

Leavis, Q.D., *Fiction and the Reading Public,* Chatto and Windus, London 1965.

Lovell, T., *Pictures of Reality: Aesthetics, Politics and Pleasure,* BFI, London 1980.

Lowenthal, L., *Literature, Popular Culture and Society,* Prentice-Hall, Englewood Cliffs, N.J. 1961.

Lukács, G., *History and Class Consciousness,* Merlin Press, London 1968.

Marx, K. and Engels, F., *The German Ideology,* Lawrence and Wishart, London 1970.

Morley, D., *The 'Nationwide' Audience,* BFI TV Monograph 11, London 1980.

Murdock, G. and Golding, P., 'For a Political Economy of Mass Communications', *Socialist Register 1973,* Merlin Press, London 1973.

Paterson, R., 'Planning the Family: the Art of the Television Schedule', *Screen Education,* No. 35, Summer 1980.

Pines, J., *Blacks in Films,* Studio Vista, London 1975.

Read, J.R., *Victorian Conventions,* Ohio UP, Athens (Ohio) 1975.

Rockwell, J., *Fact in Fiction,* Routledge and Kegan Paul, London 1974.

Rosen, M., *Popcorn Venus: Women, Movies and the American Dream,* Peter Owen, London 1975.

Rowbotham, S., 'The Trouble with Patriarchy', *New Statesman,* 21–28 December 1979.

Scannel, P., 'The Social Eye of Television, 1946–1955', *Media, Culture and Society,* Vol. 1, No. 1, 1980.

Scholes, R. and Kellog, R., *The Nature of Narrative,* OUP, New York 1979.

Seglow, P., *Trade Unionism in Television,* Saxon House, Farnborough 1978.

Stedman, R.W., *The Serial,* University of Oklahoma Press, Norman 1977.

Thornber, R., 'Why Coronation Street Will Never Be the Susi Hush Show', *Guardian,* 16 December 1974.

Timpanaro, S., *On Materialism,* New Left Books, London 1976.

Todorov, T., *The Fantastic,* Cornell UP, Cornell 1975.

Warren, T., *I Was Ena Sharples' Father,* Duckworth, London 1969.

Williams, C. (ed.), *Realism and the Cinema,* Routledge and Kegan Paul, London 1980.

Williams, R., *Culture and Society,* Chatto and Windus, London 1958.

Williams, R., *The Country and the City,* Chatto and Windus, London 1973.

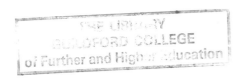

THE LIBRARY
GUILDFORD COLLEGE
of Further and Higher Education

Selected Further Reading

Alvarado, M., 'Eight Hours Are Not a Day (and Afterword)', in Rayns, T. (ed.), Fassbinder, BFI, London 1979.

Cantor, M.G., 'Our Days and Our Nights on TV', Journal of Communication, Autumn 1979.

Collins, R. and Porter, V., WDR and the Arbeiterfilm, BFI, London 1981, Chapter 5.

Edmondson, M. and Rounds, D., The Soaps, Stein and Day, New York 1973.

Gordon, N., My Life at Crossroads, W.H. Allen, London 1975.

La Guardia, R., From Ma Perkins to Mary Hartman, Ballantine, New York 1977.

de Lauretis, T., 'A Semiotic Approach to Television as Ideological Apparatus', in Newcomb, H. (ed.), Television: the Critical View, OUP, New York 1979.

Merck, M. and Wyver, J., 'Confused? You Will Be!', Time Out, No. 531, 20–26 June 1980.

Modleski, T., 'The Search for Tomorrow in Today's Soap Operas', Film Quarterly, Fall 1977.

Phoenix, P., All My Burning Bridges, Star Books, London 1976.

Stedman, R.W., The Serial, University of Oklahoma Press, Norman 1977.

Stern, L., 'Oedipal Opera: "The Restless Years" ', Australian Journal of Screen Theory, No. 4, 1978.

Warren, T., I Was Ena Sharples' Father, Duckworth, London 1969.

Weatherby, W.J., 'Granada's Camino Real', Contrast, Summer 1962.

THE LIBRARY
GUILDFORD COLLEGE
of Further and Higher Education

Author DYER, Richard et al
Television monograph

Title Coronation Street

Class 791 . 456 DYE

Accession 88814.

88814